J. B. SPENCE

THE
LIFE
OF A
TRIAL
LAWYER

Note for Librarians: A cataloguing record for this book is available from Library and Archives Canada at www.collectionscanada.ca/amicus/index-e.html
ISBN 1-4120-5257-2

PUBLISHING™
Offices in Canada, USA, Ireland and UK
This book was published *on-demand* in cooperation with Trafford Publishing. On-demand publishing is a unique process and service of making a book available for retail sale to the public taking advantage of on-demand manufacturing and Internet marketing. On-demand publishing includes promotions, retail sales, manufacturing, order fulfilment, accounting and collecting royalties on behalf of the author.

Book sales for North America and international:
Trafford Publishing, 6E–2333 Government St.,
Victoria, BC V8T 4P4 CANADA
phone 250 383 6864 (toll-free 1 888 232 4444)
fax 250 383 6804; email to orders@trafford.com
Book sales in Europe:
Trafford Publishing (UK) Limited, 9 Park End Street, 2nd Floor
Oxford, UK OXI IHH UNITED KINGDOM
phone 44 (0)1865 722 113 (local rate 0845 230 9601)
facsimile 44 (0)1865 722 868; info.uk@trafford.com
Order online at:
www.trafford.com/robots/05-0152.html

10 9 8 7 6 5 4

CONTENTS

I dedicate this book to my four wonderful children,
Mark, Martha, John and Gary.

Let reverence for the laws be breathed by every American mother to the lisping babe that prattles on her lap. Let it be taught in schools, in seminaries, and in colleges. Let it be written in primers, spelling books, and in almanacs. Let it be preached from the pulpit, proclaimed in legislative halls, and enforced in the courts of justice. And, in short, let it become the political religion of the nation.

Abraham Lincoln

CHAPTER 1

My Childhood

The most tragic event in my life was the loss of my mother when I was 12. She was killed in an automobile accident, leaving me, as her oldest child; a younger brother and two much younger sisters. All of this took place in Oklahoma City.

My father was absent, and no one knew where he was. My father did not attend the funeral. I was the only child who did, and my memory is so clear of what took place at that funeral, it is as if it happened one hour ago. I was unable to shed a tear, and there is not a day that goes by that I do not think of my mother. I don't understand all of the psychological and emotional attachments that I have today. I can only say that her death was an enormous loss.

I had a marvelous childhood with my parents in Oklahoma City. It was Depression time, and most of America was out of work. I recall my mother answering the back door to find a hungry man there and her sharing our food with him. She gave him a warm biscuit and some hash brown potatoes. When he knocked at the back door, he had taken his hat off and put it on his chest. I won't forget this scene.

This was a time when you could see a movie for 10 cents; a Coca-Cola cost a nickel, a hamburger a nickel. Everyone we knew was of modest means. However, I had a rich, full life because of my mother. She was a small woman with dark hair and brown eyes and an olive complexion. She taught Sunday school, and I was there all of the time, along with my brother, Lester, and my sisters, Darlene and Jean. She was a wonderful cook. She was a true leader. She taught me table manners. I was to say, "Yes, Ma'am," and "No, Ma'am," and "Please" and "Thank you," and never interrupt adults.

My mother had an unusual name, Pansy Pearl. Her sisters were Ruby and Betsy. I understand they were all born in Arkansas. My mother was strict and promised me that if I got in trouble at school and I got spanked by the principal that I would get another spanking when I got home. She tolerated no foolishness. I was promised that if I said a dirty word that my mouth would be washed out with soap. She was the guiding influence in my life.

In our backyard, I had a tree fort. I was an avid reader, and a bookstore close by would give me old copies of the Zane Grey novels and Ranch Romances novels. All of these stories were about white hats and black hats, good cowboys and bad cowboys, and the good ones always won. They were interesting, exciting and I enjoyed them. Some days I would spend all afternoon in that tree fort, and my mother would come out, and I would lower a basket, and she would put lunch there for me.

The laundry was done in an old-fashioned washing machine that had a wringer attached to it. I would help her with the laundry and push the clothes through the wringer to dry them and then help her hang them in the backyard in the sunshine. All of these sheets had a fresh smell after being dried in the sunshine and the fresh air.

My mother washed the dishes, I dried them. I was her junior partner.

I helped with my brother and sisters and I was encouraged to study. There were a lot of books in our home, magazines, and we got a daily newspaper. I read all of these avidly. Actually, I won a prize in the sixth grade as the best reader in Oklahoma City. I have so many memories that I could recount them forever.

On May Day, we had an event at school dancing around a may pole. My mother made a homemade uniform for me. I was a peppermint candy stick, white and red stripes. My first date, if you can call it that, was with a classmate named Dorothy who had dark hair, wore glasses and had bangs. We went to the movies together. I sat with my hands locked in my lap, petrified that if I touched her, God would punish me. To this day, every woman that I meet who has glasses, dark hair and bangs reminds me of Dorothy.

Much of the time, my father was gone. When he was home, he was very strict. He had been in the Marine Corps in World War I and had sustained serious injuries. He was a tall man, blonde with blue eyes. He was stern, aloof and distant. I do not recall my father ever telling me in my life that he loved me.

I learned to work in Oklahoma City. My mother arranged for me to have a *Saturday Evening Post* magazine route. The magazines were delivered to my home with a canvas bag to carry them in, and usually there was a Norman Rockwell painting on the front cover. It was a simplistic time and all of his covers were beautiful. In addition to the *Saturday Evening Post* route, I had a small paper route for a newspaper called *Grit*.

The *Saturday Evening Post* cost a nickel, and I went door-to-door trying to sell it, talking always to adults. There was a lady in the neighborhood who made homemade candy. I would carry that to the lumber yard, the gas stations and throughout the neighborhood trying to sell her candy. Candy salesman, paper salesman, magazine salesman. I also gathered Coke bottles in the alleys and sold them.

After my mother's death, my grandmother placed Lester, Darlene, Jean and me on a train for Sampson, Alabama, where my father had a sister, my Aunt Dolly. When she took us to the train station, she took me aside and gave me a huge basket of sandwiches and fruit and a stern lecture. She told me, "J. B., you are the oldest. You are now responsible for your family, your brother and your sisters."

No one knew where my father was. The train ride to Sampson, Alabama, was a time of fear and anxiety. My brother and sisters and I had no idea what the future held for us. We were leaving our home and going to meet a stranger. It was a long, sad train ride. Even today, when I hear a train whistle, I'm reminded of that trip.

My Aunt Dolly and her husband were warm and generous people. They met us at the train station and took us into their home. My uncle also was a World War I veteran and had serious disabilities, so we were under very modest circumstances. There was not a lot of food and here they were, with their own children, taking in four more children.

I remember Sampson, Alabama, as unfriendly. I was a stranger at the school and felt very unwelcome. I have no pleasant memories of Sampson, Alabama.

I do remember the sound of a train whistling day and night. I know that my Aunt Dolly had a huge icebox that you put ice in, and you put a pan under the bottom of the icebox to catch the melted ice. The iceman came with a horse and wagon and with a huge ice pick. He would chop off 25 pounds of ice and place it in the house in the icebox. The horse stayed in place while he did what he had to do. He put a slab on the horse's reins so he couldn't move. All of the kids in the neighborhood would scramble into the wagon getting the chips of ice.

After staying with my Aunt Dolly for a few months, my father got us. We now moved to a little town in North Florida called Baker. Here I met my grandparents for the first time.

We lived in Baker a short while and then moved out into the country into a sharecropper's house. This was an old, wooden house with no electricity, no running water, no indoor plumbing, a huge fireplace and a wood-burning kitchen stove. We had a kerosene lamp for after dark, no radio, no TV, no newspaper, no automobile. We were dirt poor.

The people who had a huge farm assigned my family as a sharecropper a number of acres of land to tend. My father was to plant cotton and corn and peanuts and raise it and turn it over to the landlord, who would, in turn, sell it and give us part of the profit.

I spent much of my time plowing a mule in the field barefoot from sunup to sundown with a break for lunch. At lunchtime, they would ring a big bell. I would unhitch the mule and ride her in for lunch.

My life at this time was work, work, work, picking cotton, pulling up peanuts, picking corn, sawing down pine trees, sawing them into blocks of wood and then with an ax chopping the block of wood into the fire wood.

I was in another world, uneducated and with a very narrow vision. The pleasure was three meals a day and lots of work.

We had an ox cart that I would drive into the woods to gather firewood. When we would have a rainstorm, after the rain I would run as fast as I could down a sandy road. Why? I don't know. Just the freedom of a run.

I learned that I had about eight uncles. I can't recall all of their names. There was Floyd, Prentiss, John, Burley and Colin that I can recall. They were all uneducated sharecroppers. My Uncle Colin raised bird dogs, and that was his sole means of support.

My father showed up one day with a young lady just a few years older than me, who was my new stepmother. Her name was Lilly Mae, and she was kind and generous and never said a harsh word to me. I did all I could to help her. She was only with us for a few months. Then we left this place and I went to live with my grandparents. They had a much nicer place.

At the first home, we didn't have a well or a pump. I would have to walk about a half-mile to the big farmer's well and carry back two buckets of water. All of the water was brought to our house like that.

My grandparents had a well, an outhouse, and it was a lot roomier. They also had a lot of chickens, hogs and wonderful food. Life changed a great deal for me. My Uncle Colin taught me how to hunt rabbits, squirrels and quail, and I did.

I had to ride a school bus from this farm to the school in Baker. I went to school barefoot. I carried my lunch every day, usually a ham sandwich and a sweet potato. My grandparents had a smokehouse, where they kept all of the ham, smoked ham and huge barrels of sugarcane syrup. They also had a sugar mill, where the sugarcane would be pushed into a huge squeezing device. The cane juice would come out on the other side and go into a large vat to become cooked into sugarcane syrup.

We had cows, chickens, hogs and lots of food. My grandmother made cornbread that was incredible. Many times I would come home from school, get a 22 rifle, a handful of shells, a large chunk of cornbread and head off into the woods to hunt.

Not too far from us was a big creek. All of us swam in the creek. Occasionally you would see a cottonmouth water moccasin. We didn't really understand that the snake was a killer, extremely poisonous.

I visited a number of my relatives from time to time. I would hitchhike from Baker, Florida, to Sopchoppy and Chattahoochee and Wakulla. Hardly anyone would pass you by in those days.

After Baker, Florida, and this farm, we moved to a place called Niceville. We were only there a short time, but I remember the move. Everything we owned was piled in a truck. I rode on top of our possessions, and it was like a scene from the *Grapes of Wrath*. Everyone stared at us.

I felt like a total foreigner, but I found work here. At age 15, I was a caddy at the golf course, and I pumped gas at the gas station. I think gasoline was about 15 cents a gallon. I also worked at a bar behind the gas station, washing the glasses, squeezing the lemons and being the bartender's juvenile assistant.

Attached to the bar was a gambling room with a crap table. The folks would gather there drinking, shooting dice and playing poker. I recall one woman. She looked like my friend, Dorothy—the dark hair, the glasses, the olive complexion, and she was wearing a blue velvet dress.

After Niceville we went to Florala, Alabama. I had a new stepmother, Margie. She was much older than Lilly Mae, but she was a very nice person. She never said a harsh word to me and I tried my best to help her.

My father was a mystery to me. I knew he had been injured in World War I, but he would never talk about it. My father received a government check for his disability the 1st of every month. We would go to town, he and I, and the routine was the same. First, we would buy groceries, basic staples. Next, my father would buy a bottle of whiskey and start drinking.

Soon, he would be very much under the influence of alcohol. Many times, he would pass out. I had the job of finding a truck and a driver to take us home. All of this was very hard. Many times he would play his harmonica, the same songs, "Turkey in the Straw" and "Red Wings."

My father would sit on the porch in a rocking chair, silent and rocking for hours. He smoked a great deal of roll-your-own Bull Durham tobacco. He could make a cigarette with one hand. My father wasn't cruel or harsh. He was very strict and quiet. He is still a mystery.

After some time in Florala, Alabama, we moved to Tallahassee, Florida, and I started attending Leon High School. We lived at 710 Dent Street in colored town. We were the only white family on that street. We we had no indoor plumbing, but we did have water and electricity.

Once more I was working. I had a paper route, the *Tallahassee Democrat*. I worked nights and weekends at a drive-in place called the Coffee Pot. People would drive up in their car and give me their order, and I would bring it to them on a tray and hook the tray on the side of the car. Beer was a dime, hamburgers a nickel. I always felt it was awkward when I waited on some of my classmates. They had dates, a car and money, and I was their curb hop.

I had difficulty going to school. I lived across town and I had no transportation other than a bicycle and a long ride to school, a long ride to the Coffee Pot, and I also had an early morning paper route.

I delivered the paper, the *Tallahassee Democrat*, to the governor's mansion. His daughter was a classmate. Tallahassee was much better than the farm, but I still felt like a foreigner. I dated two girls in high school, both redheads, both cheerleaders. One was Bertha and the other was Nell.

My father spoke to me when we arrived in Tallahassee. I believe I was about 14 or 15. He told me, in a calm voice, that from that day forward, I was to support myself. I was welcome to stay at home at 710 Dent Street, but if I needed shoes, clothes, a dentist or a haircut, they were all my responsibility. He didn't go into that much detail, but I understood what he meant.

Hitler was moving all over Europe. The *Tallahassee Democrat* put out extras frequently. I stood on the main street in Tallahassee, shouting "Extra, extra." Because of Hitler's activities, when I turned 18, I decided to join the Navy. On June 5, 1940, I enlisted in the United States Navy for six years, and this was the beginning of a fantastic chapter in my life.

CHAPTER 2

The Navy

The train ride from Tallahassee to Norfolk had me in a state of anxiety, curiosity and hope. I had joined the Navy simply to get out of Tallahassee. I didn't think I had any future interest and there was something exciting about the recruitment ad that showed a sailor and a message, "Join the Navy and See the World."

Boot camp in Norfolk was strict. We drilled for hours, every day, and we were taught how to tie knots and handle ropes. We learned the parts of the ship, the quarterdeck, the fantail, and so on. The instructor who was in charge of my group was a soft-spoken gentleman who guided us through this training. It was nothing like you see in the movies, where the instructor is in the face of the people he's trying to train, shouting vulgarities and acting in a threatening manner. I never saw anything like that. My Navy was strict, but it was also extremely respectful. In my entire six years of service, I never had anyone put a hand on me or shout at me. We respected each other, from the captain to the lowest enlisted man. Boot camp was a great learning experience for me. For some time, I was Captain of the Head (cleaning latrines spotless).

I laid awake many nights listening to one of our group playing his harmonica. He played the same song over and over, "You Are My Sunshine." This reminded me of Bertha, the cheerleader. I had promised to send her a ring.

After boot camp, I went to New London, Connecticut, and was involved in a submarine chaser training school. We were taught how to use sonar and to recognize the different sounds. When you send a sonar ping out and it struck something, you were supposed to be able to tell whether it was a whale or a submarine.

While I was in training, I spent some time on submarines. The ship that I served on in New London was the USS *Roper*, an old World War I four piper tin-can, a destroyer from World War I.

I learned later on, when starting to write this book and looking on the back of my Navy discharge, what happened to the *Roper*. In the Pacific, she was hit by a Japanese kamikaze and destroyed.

I left New London and my next stop was Key West, Florida. Here, I served on another World War I tin-can four-piper destroyer, the USS *Ruben James*. Here I was, an apprentice seaman, 21 dollars a month painting the deck, hanging over the side of the ship painting, serving as a mess cook, peeling potatoes, onions, on and on. I liked Key West. It was fun. You could get a rum and Coke after 5:00 for 35 cents and the second one for a penny.

Our duty in Key West was very simple. We left the harbor every morning along with the submarine. We proceeded to a "hunting area." The submarine would dive and then try to hide and evade us. We played cat and mouse in about a 25-mile area. When we thought we had a sonar contact, we would radio the submarine that we had a contact, drop an apple box from the stern, and the submarine would release a huge blob of oil. If we had made a successful hit, the apple box would be in the middle of the oil blob. How quaint!

I also learned from the back of my Navy discharge that this ship, the *Ruben James*, was destroyed by a German submarine in the North Atlantic long after I left her.

Everyone was friendly, and during this period of time, I learned to be a signalman. I was promoted from an apprentice seaman at 21 dollars a month, to third-class seaman at 54 dollars a month; seaman first-class at 64 dollars a month; and third class petty officer signalman at 72 dollars a month.

I was in the movies on December the 7th, 1941, in Key West when the lights were turned on and everyone was told to return to their ship or station on the double. I had no idea what was involved. My main concern was getting reimbursed the 25 cents that it cost me to get into the movie because I hadn't seen the whole film. We learned as soon as we got back to our ship that the Japanese had bombed Pearl Harbor.

We left the harbor, and went to sea. I don't think we had any ammunition and not much fuel.

As a signalman, I learned Morse code, how to send signals with a big signal light, flashing the message to another ship. I also learned all of the flags and how to hoist them to make a signal, and I learned the use of semaphore flags.

When I was learning to be a signalman apprentice, I had the 4:00 a.m. to 8:00 a.m. watch in Key West, I saw a ship sending us a message, simply calling out with a flashing light over and over. I kept giving the ship the signal to start the message, which was a K, just a simple K, dot, dash, dot. The ship wouldn't start the message. At dawn, I found out that it was a flashing sea buoy, no ship.

Before I left the *Ruben James*, we did a lot of traveling in the Caribbean. We went to Guantanamo Bay, Aruba, St. Lucia, San Juan and other places on this old World War I destroyer.

As I said, the Navy was fun, and they pulled little tricks on you. When I first got on this old destroyer, I was told by my supervisor to go down in the engine room and get a can of striped paint. I did as I was told: went down in the engine room and asked for the can of striped paint. The engine room man told me that he was out of striped paint, but if I went up to another department in the front of the ship that they had striped paint. After about an hour of going all over the ship chasing the striped paint, it dawned on me, the country boy, "J. B., there isn't such a thing as striped paint."

When things quieted down, I was bored to tears with my assignment in Key West, and I filed a request to be assigned to any ship or station in the American Navy.

Shortly, orders came back sending me to Reykjavik, Iceland, so I left Key West. I went to Boston and caught a huge cargo ship for Iceland. The North Atlantic was rough and tough, nothing like Key West.

When I arrived in Iceland, I went to the naval operating base. It had a huge sign over the entrance that read "Kwitcher Belikan." (Quit your bellyaching.) I spent the next 18 months of my life in Reykjavik, Iceland.

In the winter, there was about an hour of dawn, and in the summer about an hour of darkness, which was very confusing. We had a huge signal tower on the dock of the harbor downtown, and most of the convoy ships en route to Minsk, Russia, stopped for us for a day or two. A number of them never came back. The Germans would fly over once a week or so and give us a good scare. Iceland was no fun to me, but it surely saved my life because ships were being sunk in the North Atlantic almost daily. Iceland is still a mystery to me.

The Icelandic girls didn't like the American Navy. The Germans had been there for sometime and they related to each other so in the 18 months I was there, I had one date, and it was on my 21st birthday. I managed to get a bottle of Four Roses whiskey. Iceland was dry, not a beer, no alcohol available.

My date and I went to a big dance hall. She was taller than me, buxom and strong. We had a drink; we were dancing. Someone tapped me on the shoulder to cut in. Without looking back, I said, "Shove off, Jack, before I tag you."

With that, a big merchant marine sailor spun me around, hit me in the eye, and I went down on my knees. He quickly smacked me in the other eye. Both eyes started to close, no vision. He took my date, my bottle of Four Roses and left. Happy 21st birthday, J.B.

After 18 months, I got to come home. I was on a huge cargo ship, and because it was empty, it rolled and pitched in the Atlantic Ocean like a cork. I left the ship at Greenock, Scotland, and I caught a train to London.

London, England, in 1943 was still being bombed every night by the Germans. The sirens never quit sounding. It was scary, but I felt immune to injury, and I had a roaring good time for 30 days in London, dancing all night, drinking, partying. Incredible.

Most of the Englishmen were gone in the battle against the Germans, and the young women were anxious to have a good time. We were outnumbered 10 to one. They broke in on the dances. The main place to go was Covent Garden. They had two orchestras, one on one end and one on the other. They took turns playing. The music never stopped.

Next stop, the Brooklyn Navy Yard. I was evaluated by a psychiatrist with respect to my next assignment, and he asked me if I had a problem. I told him yes, and he said, "What is it?" I said, "Iceland was pretty lonely, and I would like to go someplace where you can see people, especially girls."

So I was sent to Miami, another submarine chaser school. A large number of our fellow students were Russians, big, blonde, blue-eyed, strong and aggressive. Then, on a blind date, I met the young woman whom I married, Patricia Edmonds. I was 21; she was 19. She was gorgeous, stunning, a brunette with brown eyes and an olive complexion.

In a sense, she reminded me of my mother. She was full of energy, just wonderful to be with. We were married in a beautiful Methodist church. She wore a long white gown and all of her family was present. I wore my dress Navy blues. I still look at that picture. It is like something out of a fairy tale, an American story.

After some time in Miami, I was reassigned to a new ship, a destroyer, the USS *Gary* stationed in Charleston, South Carolina.

I caught the USS *Gary* and started on a chapter of my life that was really tough. The *Gary* was a little over 300 feet long. I slept in a compartment with about 30 or 35 other sailors. We had a crew of a little over 200 people and we were the smallest fighting ship in the American Navy. We escorted convoys to England and to Africa, taking huge cargo ships, tankers and ammunition ships to those different ports.

We escorted convoys. A convoy was made up of 20 or 30 huge ships, and four or five destroyers were along acting as something like shepherd dogs around a herd of sheep. We were on the outside. We would circle the convoy and change positions so that we could protect them from German submarines.

Our speed was as fast as the slowest ship, which was generally 12 miles an hour. It took a long time to cross the Atlantic. The sea was very, very rough, with huge waves. It was cold; it was wet. We were constantly chasing what we thought were submarines. Many were false chases.

My assignment was on the bridge of the destroyer as a signalman sending flashing light signals by Morse code and then hoisting flags to the convoy to signal our next move. We would change course every several hours to try to elude the German submarines.

Shanghai

We zigzagged across the Atlantic. We encountered submarines. We had submarines sink some of the cargo ships, and sometimes we did not go back to pick up the survivors, if there were any. These were our orders. It was known that if you stopped or slowed down to pick up survivors, you were an easy target for the U-boats. Back and forth across the Atlantic we went, about 10 convoys.

I remember when we learned that President Roosevelt had died. The captain assembled us on the stern of our ship and read a long prayer. I had seen President Roosevelt while I was in boot camp. He rode by in an open touring car with his Panama hat on and a cigarette holder in his mouth cocked at about a 45-degree angle, and he waved to us as we stood at parade rest. They fired a 21-gun salute for the President and I stood there, farm boy, stunned that I was actually seeing in person the President of the United States.

The war ended in Europe. Convoy duty was over. We spent some time in the Boston Navy yard getting some new guns and other equipment replaced before we met our new assignment, which was the Pacific.

Upon returning to the United States after each convoy, my wife, Patricia, would join me in Brooklyn or Boston. Those days and moments were incredible. I think I was the happiest man on the face of the earth.

After our ship was refitted, we were sent to the Pacific. The war with Japan was still going on. An enormous armada of ships was gathering in the Leyte Gulf. We made a stop at Pearl Harbor and then Saipan and on to the Gulf of Leyte.

We operated six destroyers and two aircraft carriers. We were preparing for the invasion of Japan. Then an atomic bomb was dropped, and then a second atomic bomb and the Japanese surrendered.

We were close to Okinawa, and we were sent to Formosa to pick up American prisoners of war. This was a chilling moment, to see our brothers in arms so thin they couldn't walk. We transported these prisoners to the aircraft carrier. I still have photographs of the prisoners of war. When we went into Formosa we went through a minefield, dodging the mines, and we came out a different way.

The prisoners were not able to eat. When they had bread and jam and tea, they couldn't keep it down. On my wall in my office today I have photographs of these Formosa prisoners of war, our people.

Our admiral sent us a message: "For evacuating POWs from Formosa you were nothing short of sensational. Every officer and enlisted man on your ship deserves resounding applause for shoving your nose into Formosa before the occupation on a most worthy cause. The handling of passengers and their care like everything else in the operation was done in the American way and there is no better. I pass to you the Seventh Fleet's message, 'Your proven determined action in Formosa under difficult circumstances was a magnificent and difficult performance and a Godsend to our prisoners. Well done. Admiral Kincaid'."

I still treasure that message.

The war was over, but we still patrolled the Pacific. We wanted to be certain that it was over.

The next event in my life was a horrible typhoon in Okinawa. It is difficult to describe a typhoon. Some are very large and cover hundreds of miles. The wind can gust up as high as 150 miles an hour. The seas can be enormous, 40-, 50-foot seas. A destroyer such as the *Gary* would pitch, toss, twist, turn, dive. Seas smash you from all directions. The rain can be blinding.

If your ship rolls 70 degrees, it is likely to turn over and sink. We had a number of 60- and 65-degree rolls and the *Gary* would hang there at the brink of disaster for 15 or 20 seconds. Your heart was in your throat, death was moments away.

I prayed, and prayed, and prayed that the typhoon wouldn't kill me because I wanted to go home to the woman I loved.

After this experience, everyone on the *Gary* that had been enlisted for just the period of time of the war was eligible to go home. I had a six-year enlistment and this was September '45. I still had until June 5th of '46 to continue to serve in the American Navy. They were going home and I was staying.

We were in Hong Kong until May of '46. We would go to Shanghai once in a while and visit for the weekend. I was a money launderer in Hong Kong. The reason was that when you went ashore, you had to trade your money at a Chinese bank for Chinese money. You presented your money, and they had an abacus. They would push the beads one way or the other to show what the exchange rate was.

If your money was new and crisp, you got a higher exchange rate, so we learned to launder our money, throw it in the washing machine, add some starch, take it out and with a hot iron, press it until it was as crisp as a new deck of cards so we got a higher exchange rate.

Now occurred an enormous event in our lives. Our captain's father was an admiral in Washington and we were allowed to come home, not back across the Pacific to San Francisco, but the other way around through the Suez Canal and across the Atlantic back to Charleston, South Carolina, around the world.

We left from Shanghai, stopped in Hong Kong and then Singapore, and we spent a few days there, but before we got to Singapore, another event. We crossed the equator and the captain stopped the *Gary* on what we thought was the equator and we had an initiation that has a long history and legend in the American Navy.

If you have not crossed the equator on a Navy ship, you are a pollywog. If you have crossed the equator, you are a shellback. So the shellbacks were ready for us pathetic pollywogs, and they had rigged a huge tub perhaps 20 feet across and about three or four feet deep. It contained oil, the garbage from about a month and other matters.

It smelled to high heaven. They had rigged above the tub an oiled slope of wood, and you were forced to squat at the top of the slope, and with a huge whack, you went into the tub. You couldn't see; you were choking with the stench, and when you came out, when you could get out, they would knock you down with a fire hose.

They shaved some people's heads, put some in the brig, and a couple of folks actually got hurt. I tore my foot up on the deck and couldn't put on a shoe. I made a vow then that I would never subject myself to any other initiation for any reason if I had the choice. So in Singapore I was hopping around on crutches, and after a few days I was all right.

The next stop was Ceylon, Colombo. Now this was fun, too, and I bought a handful of zircons. They look like diamonds, and they didn't cost much, but I wanted to take them home and just give them to people. After Ceylon, Colombo, we went through the Suez Canal and we stopped at Alexandria, Egypt. There I watched some incredible belly dancers. I failed to see the pyramids, but I did ride a camel.

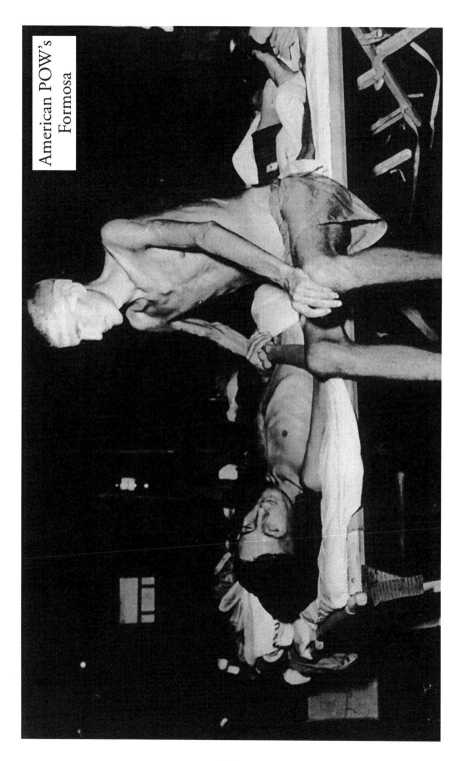

American POW's
Formosa

I failed to get back to the dock in time to catch the boat back to the *Gary* and I had to spend the night in Alexandria in an Egyptian hotel. I was so concerned that I didn't take my uniform off, not even my hat. Early the next morning, a huge Egyptian with a big white robe stopped at the doorway to wake me up. I was already awake, and he scared me good.

I went down to the dock and there was no Navy boat to pick me up. The *Gary* was sitting out in the harbor, so I gave an Egyptian in a small boat my watch to take me out to the *Gary*. As we were crossing the harbor, the *Gary* was getting under way. The anchor was up and she was slowly moving, maybe two or three miles an hour.

I had my boatman change course to go quicker, so I wouldn't be left in Egypt. All of the crew now saw me and were standing along on the deck on the side of the ship cheering me on, "Come on, Spence, come on."

My captain had some weird sense of humor. He was laughing, too, and he would nudge the *Gary* ahead just a little. Finally, I got to the *Gary*. They lowered a sea ladder, I climbed aboard. I was not chastised by anyone, including the captain.

After Egypt, the next stop was Naples. We were there for several days and some of my shipmates brought some young Italian girls on board at night from a sea ladder at the back of the *Gary*. They also had some Italian wine and they had a party.

No one seemed to notice this. None of the officers did. My shipmates were pretty secretive about it. We left Naples and the next stop was Marseilles, France. We were there for several days, but en route to Marseilles, the captain discovered the young women on board and he was furious. No one would admit this wrong, so the young ladies left us at Marseilles.

While we were in Marseilles, they had a huge military parade, and they played the French national anthem. We were invited to march in their parade, and we did. People were throwing flowers at us and clapping.

Before leaving Marseilles, I found a puppy to take home to my wife, Patricia. I named the dog Mademoiselle Pepper, and everyone loved her, wanted to take her away from me, overfed her, petted her, on and on.

Mademoiselle Pepper

We left Marseilles and headed home back through the Azores. We stopped briefly in the Azores and then headed back to our home port of Charleston, South Carolina, precisely where I had left to participate in two wars, the battle for the Atlantic and the fight for the Pacific.

I was discharged in Charleston, South Carolina. I had the puppy, Mademoiselle Pepper, and I caught the train to Richmond, Virginia, where my wife, Patricia, was waiting for me.

Our reunion in Richmond I shall never forget. Heaven on earth.

CHAPTER 3

Coming Home

I felt very much like a complete stranger coming out of the Navy and going back into civilian life. As the cars would drive by, I couldn't separate them. I didn't know which was a Ford, or which was a Chevrolet. They all looked alike.

I was living with my wife, Patricia, the little dog, Mademoiselle, and my mother-in-law, Lillian, a very warm, kind and generous person. Now was the time to go back to work and find a job, and I did.

For a while, I painted houses. Because I was a junior person, I arrived first. I put out all of the canvas, stirred all of the paint and got everything set up for the professional painters. They would give me the unpleasant assignments inside closets or under the sink with all the bugs and spiders. I would climb the ladder, I painted under the protrusion from the roof, and that job lasted sometime until they moved the jobs so far away that I couldn't get to them.

I tried to get a job with a railroad, which was somewhat of a dream. I went to the Florida East Coast Railway and applied, but nothing happened. I had had an uncle in Oklahoma who was an engineer on the railroad, and I had seen big pictures of him poised by his train. I would have liked to have worked for the railroad.

I got any kind of job that I could. I worked on a construction site as a carpenter, learning how to drive nails and build floors. That was an experience. I also mowed lawns with a push lawnmower, which had no power.

Then I tried to get a job with the police department. They were not hiring either. I worked in a hardware store selling batteries and tires and screwdrivers and so on. My next effort was driving a laundry truck, picking up people's laundry and dry-cleaning and bringing it back.

A lot of these folks didn't have money to pay me or said they didn't, and I would still deliver their laundry and dry-cleaning. They said they would pay me next time. That job didn't last very long.

So I went to see the Veterans Administration's representative. He told me I was going to continue to be a peasant until I got some education, so I enrolled in the Lindsay Hopkins night school in downtown Miami. In October of 1947, I received my high school diploma, but my employment opportunities did not improve.

I worked in a car lot trying to sell used cars, but that didn't help much, so I went back to see the Veterans Administration's representative again, who encouraged me to get a year or two of college.

So I went out to the University of Miami and I took a placement test. They gave me in one day 15 college credits. Incredible. I couldn't believe it. So I stayed and acquired 60 college credits.

A friend of mine ran a gas station, and he suggested I go to law school. I had never met a lawyer. I had never been in Court. I had never seen a judge. I was totally ignorant about what a lawyer does.

My friend kept encouraging me. He told me I could get a job, he thought, after graduation, with the government, maybe the FBI. So on his encouragement with 60 college credits and no LSAT, I enrolled in the law school at the University of Miami.

On the first day, the Dean came around to the freshman class and told us to look at the person on the right and the one on the left. He said after the first semester, they wouldn't be there, so I was full of fear, fear of failure, fear of being in over my head, really frightened. The Veterans Administration paid for my books, which were a stack about three feet high, and they paid for my tuition, plus I received 105 dollars a month.

My wife, Patricia, did her part and more. She had a job in Coral Gables, working as a bookkeeper. She was my complete partner in every respect. I worked on weekends bagging groceries at a grocery store in Coral Gables, but I did study the law very hard.

I have often told the story about how I geared myself to study. I would study for hours until I thought that's where the C students would be. Then I would go longer, to where I thought the B students would be. Then I would keep studying, and go on more until I thought I was where the A students would be, and sometimes I would go beyond that.

I found the law fascinating. Reading the cases was actually easy for me. After the first semester our grades were posted and incredibly, I had made straight A's. I couldn't believe it.

I made friends with the folks who I thought were the brightest students. I was invited to become a member of the *Law Review* and on February 5, 1951, I graduated magna cum laude.

I was sworn in as a member of the Florida Bar by a Circuit Court judge in his office during the lunch hour, just the judge and me. At that time, we didn't have to take a Florida Bar exam, and I was now a member of the Florida Bar.

A very distinguished Attorney General, Richard Ervin, had a program of inviting graduating students, one or two, from each of the law schools in Florida. I had served as president of the law school student body and had been initiated into the highest honor society in our school. Richard Ervin invited me to come to Tallahassee and serve as a special Assistant Attorney General for the State of Florida, a miracle.

So Patricia and I moved to Tallahassee, found a small apartment, and I went to work for the first time as a lawyer, sitting in a huge room with about 25 or 30 other young special assistants reading Florida Statutes, incredibly boring.

While in law school, a prominent attorney came to speak to the entire law school student body. He spoke at the Miracle Theater in downtown Coral Gables. This gentleman was Perry Nichols. He stood on stage for about an hour-and-a-half talking about trial tactics, trying a case, preparation, opening statements, direct examination, cross examination, exhibits and final arguments. His talk was spellbinding. I was in complete awe of this man.

Incredibly, Mr. Nichols came to Tallahassee. The Legislature was in session, and he was concerned about what the Legislature might pass that would affect his field of practice, personal injury law.

I walked up to him in the hallway of the Legislature. He was a big man, over six feet tall, heavy-set with a deep voice. He was wearing a seersucker suit, which was very stylish then, and black and white shoes.

I introduced myself and told him about hearing him at the Miracle Mile Theatre and that I would very much like to work for him. He asked me a few questions about my background and the simple question: "Will you work?"

I told him a little bit about my farm background, about serving in the Navy and that I would be thrilled to work with him. He walked away saying, "I'll let you know."

About a week later, I received a phone call from Mr. Nichols. He told me he had checked me out with the Attorney General, Richard Ervin, and that I was highly recommended. He told me that he was mailing me a plane ticket to Miami, and he was going to hire me.

He also told me that I would have lunch with him and his partners when I got to Miami and I was to say nothing to them but yes, sir and no, sir. So for the first time in my life, I got on an airplane in May of '51 and flew to Miami.

There was a dry cleaning place in downtown Miami. I went there upon my arrival and stood in a barrel in my underwear while they pressed my suit. With a crew cut, white Panama hat, and suit pressed so sharp that the crease would almost cut, I went to Mr. Nichols' office and had lunch with him and his partners. I was hired for 4,800 dollars a year. I had no concept of what I was going to do.

Patricia and I drove to Miami, rented a little one-room garage apartment almost identical to the one we lived in all the time that I was in law school. Once more, I was full of fear. I knew absolutely nothing about practicing law.

Each assignment that I received was brand new. I was also given the task of coming in every Saturday and going through all of the closed files and pulling out the legal memos. I did that and read each one and built a legal memo file that taught me a lot.

I lived in fear for this first year or so, knowing that at any day I could be fired because I didn't think I was doing anything that helped, but each of the partners was a complete gentleman. Each of them was helpful. Each one briefed me on the assignments, and slowly I caught on. I started filing lawsuits, going to motion calendars and taking depositions.

I remember the first deposition as clearly as if it happened today. Our client was a little elderly lady who was hurt on a bench in an amusement park that collapsed. The defendant's attorney was the senior defense lawyer in Miami.

When we arrived at his office for the deposition, my shirt was plastered to me. I could barely speak. The office was downtown in a big building with no air conditioning and all the windows open with no screens. Near his desk was a huge brass spittoon.

He only asked about 20 questions and we were out of there, but slowly I learned. I came in early, I stayed late, I read everything I could get my hands on, and a wonderful life developed.

Patricia and I were able to buy our first home in Hialeah for 9,500 dollars, a brand new sparkling, two-bedroom CBS house with hardwood floors. She was still working, my full partner and helper, and she was a wonderful, loving wife. I rode two buses to work.

Then we had our first child, Mark, and two years later our second child, Martha. We were living a fairytale life, the American dream. We moved to South Miami, a new home with a swimming pool, and we all had the material things of financial success. We went to church every Sunday with our children. We were a close-knit family with much affection and fun.

Sadly, Patricia became ill. She suffered a long illness and death. I had two small children, ages 10 and 8. My world was in turmoil with confusion and guilt. I had not understood Patricia's illness and, looking back, I had not been as helpful as I could have been.

Slowly, I started rebuilding my life. I met a wonderful woman, an airline stewardess, Mary Jo Kruse. We became friends and more than that. She was a remarkable woman. In addition to being an airline stewardess, she had a real estate agency. She was a tomboy, wore her hair in a ponytail and played golf sometimes barefoot; we went quail hunting together, and she was a better shot than me. If I went fishing, she was clearly a much better fisherman than me. A lot of fun. She was a small woman, with beautiful dark hair, dark eyes and somewhat of an olive complexion, very bright, a very well-read college graduate.

After some time, we were married and she, through some connection with the airlines, arranged an incredible trip for our honeymoon. We started from the St. Regis Hotel in New York and went to Lisbon, Portugal, then to Madrid, Barcelona, the Island of Majorca, Naples, Zurich, Paris and London. Incredible.

We had a wonderful life as a close family for many years. Mary Jo and I had two sons, John and Gary. We had a magnificent home in Miami on property a block long in length from one avenue to another, a gorgeous pool, tennis court, several boats, a rose garden, a yard full of dogs, like something out of a movie.

Time went on. Mark and Martha went off to college, then John and Gary. I was a very busy fellow practicing law.

Perry Nichols told us that when his son, Richard, graduated from law school that he was going to leave the firm and practice with his son, so we each had to open our own law firm. I told my two partners that I had enough money to finance us for one year and we had to get it done in a year. We opened an office downtown.

Now I was virtually on my own. I didn't have all of the money that we had at the Nichols firm, I didn't have a line of credit; I didn't have a name that would attract business. This once more was a scary time.

We took every case that we were offered, and I embarked on a very hectic life. I tried cases all over the State of Florida, from Key West to Tallahassee, West Palm Beach, Ft. Lauderdale, Tampa, St. Petersburg, Bartow, Punta Gorda, Melbourne, and in other states, Louisiana and Georgia.

I had a frantic existence. On one occasion, I overdosed on sleeping pills. I would wake up sometimes in a Holiday Inn and for a moment actually did not know where I was. I generally had an investigator with me and sometimes a partner, but many of these cases I tried alone.

And I can tell you a Miami lawyer is not very welcome in many of these cities. The judge is suspicious because you're from Miami, and opposing counsel has probably gone to high school with the judge or played football with him, and now he's regularly playing golf with him. So you felt like you had one strike against you when you walked in, and you had to be on your absolute best behavior and be totally prepared to do your best.

In spite of my legal life, I continued to have a great life with my family.

We made many trips to the Bahamas, to San Francisco, to Vermont, Homosassa Springs. I coached Little League baseball. I bought a bunch of books on how to be a baseball coach and had a great time.

I bought a huge batting cage for my backyard and a batting machine that would throw baseballs. Every young boy in the neighborhood was in that cage. My sons were fishing, and winning every award that you could win. We had a home down in the Keys in Islamorada. My son, Mark, and Martha won many awards. They were straight-A students and achieved real distinction in all of their efforts.

Many things were happening to me. I served on the Constitution Revision Commission and we met frequently in Tallahassee in the old Senate chambers. On my desk to my immediate right was former Governor Leroy Collins, and on my left was the Chief Justice of the Florida Supreme Court, B. K. Roberts.

This was an exciting time. Both of my sons came up and served as pages. To sit and watch my sons walk across the Senate floor was humbling, to say the least.

The Dade County judges and lawyers voted me as the top trial lawyer in Miami, topped off with a big, wonderful story in the paper.

Perry Nichols played an enormous role in my life. He sent me a letter telling me he was as proud of me as if I were one of his sons. I'll treasure that letter forever. He practically adopted me because I was the peasant in many hierarchies, and he had come from a farm background himself.

Time flew; years went by. I was a busy man, and I loved doing what I was doing. Slowly, things changed. Mary Jo and I were home alone. She had always been interested in fishing. I had purchased her a good-sized boat, 27 or 28 feet long. She hurt her leg on that boat, so we got her a huge Hatteras, the *Mary Jo II.*

She spent a lot of time in Bimini. She became the Commodore of the Big Game Fishing Club. She had a life of her own with me and all of our children gone, and we quietly decided to end our marriage. We did. It was calm, polite, no harsh words. We agreed on everything and wished each other good luck.

Recently, Mary Jo passed away. She had been ill for some time. Everyone who knew her will miss her because she played such a great role in many people's lives. All four of my children were blessed to have her as their mother.

CHAPTER 4

History

Many people ask me what it was like to practice law in the fifties. That seems like a very long time ago, and indeed, great changes have occurred, but I would like to share with you some thoughts from a good friend, Frank Howard, who wrote a beautiful article for *The Dade County Bar Bulletin*. Some of his comments are worth looking at.

"There was one courthouse, the 1925 vintage building on Flagler Street, for almost all civil and criminal proceedings. It was the skyscraper of downtown. The long, spacious lobby had not long since been concealed by primitive air-conditioning work resulting in the current campaign to preserve its height and balcony.

"The jail was on the 15th floor. The two drinking fountains on each floor were clearly marked 'White' and 'Colored.'

"Judges' offices and some courtrooms had windows, air-conditioning units, and there were a few spittoons around. The FEC Railway terminal was a block away, and many a trial had to be suspended while a train arrived.

"There weren't many judges and each had his method and his quirks, the sources of study and gossip. Most counties in Florida had one Circuit Court judge or shared a judge with another county in the same circuit. Dade had a grand total of six sitting Circuit Court judges: Marshall Wisehart, who lived up to his name, Vernon Hawthorne, a veteran of the First World War who was soon to retire; Stanley Milledge, an unabashed liberal who lived to philosophize and was always worth listening to; Charles Carroll, the temperamental Harvardian who was rumored in his days to have driven off a pier into Biscayne Bay while in the grips of demon rum, who later graced the District Court of

Appeals and, finally, George Holt, an autocratic figure much feared and frowned upon."

Pat Cannon, a later Circuit judge who weighed around 350 pounds, often fell asleep on the bench and generated dozens of anecdotes, was said to have remarked about Holt, "Oh, I know George Holt, and I think he's honest. Of course, he's no fanatic about it."

I tried cases in front of all of these judges. They were very polite and considerate, and, in my view, great judges.

Today it is vastly different. We have over 100 Circuit Court judges in Dade County, and many of them I have never seen.

Frank also added this paragraph: "A sea of change took place in tort litigation when Perry Nichols formed a partnership with some of the best trial lawyers in town, hired first-class investigators and medical experts and developed artistic charts and graphs and dramatic bags of tricks to flourish before juries. This group began winning verdicts in the hundreds of thousands, unheard of before, and collecting contingency fees, which made them rich and the defense bar apoplectic with envy.

"The insurance companies, unused to serious competition, masked their fury with grave pronouncements suggesting these scandalous dogs were a sign of moral decay, and the American way of life was at risk."

A lot can be said about the Perry Nichols' firm because at that time, it was a giant, not only in Miami, but across the nation. Our first office was tiny, and we soon outgrew it. Eventually, we built a round building on Brickell, which later became the Channel 6 building. The architecture was very modern, over five stories high, not including the ground level, and 10 specialty divisions, each of which housed an older lawyer, a younger lawyer and two secretaries and an investigator.

The divisions were aviation, medical, railroad, appellate, etcetera. We hired a full-time doctor and put him through law school. There were over 100 people working in our offices of Tampa, Ft. Lauderdale and Orlando.

The firm had a medical library, photographers, a darkroom, visual aids, movies, videos, manuals, medical journals, and all of the other latest equipment. Each division had its own specialty library. It was very efficient and very well-organized. Nichols had a lot of imagination and it stunned America.

In 1967, the firm separated on very friendly terms. Perry and his son, Richard, went alone, forming their own office and did well. It was amazing what happened with all the other members from the Perry Nichols firm.

From it emerged five judges, chief judges, three presidents of the American Trial Lawyers, two presidents of the International Society of Barristers, four presidents of the International Academy of Trial Lawyers, six presidents of the Academy of Florida Trial Lawyers, and nine members of the Inner Circle of Advocates.

Perry was a giant. He was a combination of Billy Graham, Vince Lombardi and George Patton. He was a marvelous leader. I remember that once a year, the partners would meet to discuss raises for all of the young associates, and Perry always insisted that we give them more. The bulk of that came from his part. We were a team, and he was our leader.

This man was a giant in my life. He took me hunting, quail hunting, on his ranch. He took me fishing. I spent time with him at his house in Stiltsville. We used to hunt and shoot, trap and skeet together. If I am a good lawyer today, it is because I had the great fortune to be part of Perry Nichols' team.

We never handled medical malpractice cases. We did not want to destroy the good will of the medical community, which were always testifying in our cases. But one case came along that we simply couldn't turn down. It involved a Mrs. Holl. She went into the Victoria Hospital for a simple hemorrhoidectomy. There was no problem with the surgery, but post-surgery, she was grossly overmedicated by the wrong medicines and it rendered her permanently and totally paralyzed, needing 24-hour-a-day care. Her husband abandoned her, leaving her with several small children. Her very elderly mother was doing her best to take care of her.

We took this case, filed it and the trial court dismissed it. We took an appeal, and the Supreme Court ruled that we were entitled to a jury trial.

Holl vs. Talcott is a leading case in Florida law on the right to have a jury rule in a medical malpractice case. We tried this case, and under the rules at that time the defendant could ask that the Court appoint a physician to review the records, examine the patient and testify.

A local doctor was appointed by the judge. He read the records, examined Mrs. Holl, and in his opinion, there was gross negligence on the part of the doctors and the hospital.

This physician was extremely reluctant to testify. He knew that he would be hurt in the medical community if he testified and gave his opinion. He begged to be let off, so our trial judge called him as the Court's witness and questioned him on the medical negligence.

His testimony was powerful and persuasive, and the jury rendered a verdict of $1.5 million, the very first million-dollar verdict in the State of Florida.

The phone was ringing off the hook in my office. Everyone who thought they had a medical malpractice case wanted to see me. The publicity was incredible, all over the newspapers, all over TV, on and on.

I now had a new problem. I couldn't pronounce the medical words that described what was wrong or had gone wrong with all of these new clients with potential medical malpractice cases: Congenital anomaly, retrolental fibroplasias, succinylcholine, Volkmann's contracture, endotracheal tube, Pitocin.

I needed a new education. I hired two retired doctors to help me. I attended medical seminars. I subscribed to all of the medical journals. The president of the American Trial Lawyers appointed me chairman of the medical malpractice committee for that national organization. I also served as President of the American Board of Professional Liability Attorneys. I was invited to give talks on ABC, NBC and CBS.

Connie Chung came to my house in Islamorada. I'll never forget that lady. She had on white jeans, white sneakers, T-shirt, and the most beautiful wedding ring I have ever seen in my life. It was a wide gold ring with many tiny diamonds in it. It was like something in the sky. My family was petrified with Connie Chung in our house. All of this was great fun.

People were almost standing in line to get in my office the first year that I made a million dollars. I had made only 980,000 dollars, and two of my partners gave me 10,000 dollars each so I could brag, if I wanted to, that I had made a million dollars.

I can't help but think of that boy plowing that mule in the field and that kid in the Navy peeling potatoes and onions for 21 dollars a month, but it wasn't all peaceful.

I had represented a lady in Ft. Lauderdale and got a million-dollar-plus verdict for her. She was a widow with small children, but she had a boyfriend who was Jamaican, and the lawyers who originally had the case had promised that Jamaican person a big portion of any recovery that was made. I was unaware of this.

After the trial, this person came to me and demanded the empty promise that had been made to him. Under the law, the Court ruled he was not entitled to anything. Shortly thereafter, I received a phone call in my office from a woman with a cultivated voice who told me, "Mr. Spence, I represent the Jamaican Shower Posse, and we're going to bomb your home." I tried to ask her why but she hung up.

A few days later the same person called me at home on Key Biscayne and gave me the same message, "We're going to bomb your home."

I contacted the police, and they knew a great deal about the Jamaican Shower Posse, how ruthless and vicious they were. They posted security at my home, tapped the phone and finally the threats went away.

In one of my national TV appearances, the interviewer was a woman and we were sitting in my office with cameras running. To my total surprise, she reached in her briefcase and handed me the letter that the previous attorneys had given to the Jamaican. In the letter, the promise was made. She put the letter in front of me and asked me what I thought about it.

Here I was on national TV, with this piece of terrible evidence in my face, and I reached back as deep as I could and kept an expressionless face and told her I had never seen it, that it was without merit, and the Jamaican could take it to the judge, but under the law, he had no claim.

I was invited to Washington to debate one of the representatives of the American Medical Association. We were very, very busy. We had a huge caseload and we were trying lots of cases.

A Dominican Airlines plane leaving the Miami Airport had some kind of engine trouble and tried to get back to the airport, but crashed on 36th Street. A huge ball of fire landed in the back yard of the Knapp family, burning alive their two teenage sons.

I tried that case, and the jury verdict was $1.8 million. Once more, national publicity. I even received letters from lawyers in London asking how on earth could a jury have rendered a verdict of 1.8 million dollars for the death of a child.

One of the most telling events in that case was the appearance of a vice-president of the Dominican Airlines, who was called as a defense witness. He was a handsome man, very polished, very well-dressed. He looked like Harry Belafonte, charming, but he didn't speak English, so we had a drawn-out, laborious procedure.

The question was asked in crisp English, translated to Spanish; the answer was given in Spanish and then transferred back into English. Slow, long, drawn-out and somewhat confusing. I cross-examined the vice-president for a long time and finally he lost his temper and blurted out, "I am not a mechanic, I'm a vice-president." And he said it in English.

The jury sat up like they had been hit by a bolt of lightning, and the ballgame was over. Unbelievable. All credibility the defense had had evaporated.

These are things that happen in Court that you can't plan on. I don't know whether it's luck, persistence or what, but I'm glad it happened.

Another case. Once more we had established a record. The Knapp verdict was the largest verdict in America for the death of a teenager. On appeal, it was approved and then we tried the second case involving the other son who was burned alive. This time the airline's lawyers were smart. They admitted liability. There was only one issue before the jury, and Mr. Belafonte did not come back. This verdict: 800,000 dollars.

The next case that I had involved the death of a child, an 8-year-old boy named Jamie Kaylor. They were building a new home adjacent to his home, and all the children in the neighborhood played in and around the construction. They were virtually invited there by the workmen, and in the process of building this new home, a 13-ton pile of white sand was delivered to the construction site.

Young Jamie dug a hole in the sand pile when it collapsed and killed him.

The Kaylors asked me to represent them for their son's death. I told them I didn't how to win the lawsuit. How could I criticize the construction people? The only criticism I could think of was construction people should have put a sign on the sand pile, "Keep Out," but I didn't think a jury would accept that as being any kind of negligence.

The next thought I had was security to have someone there to shoo the children away. I didn't think that that would work either.

The last thought I had was to build some kind of fence around the sand pile, but none of these I thought would amount to negligence. I told the Kaylors I couldn't represent them, and they went away.

A couple of months later they came back, and said they would pay me up front if I would represent them, win or lose, and I changed my mind. I said, "I'll handle the case on the regular contingency fee basis. If we're successful, we get paid, and if we're not, there's no fee."

During the trial, the defendant contractor was on the stand, and I asked him if they had any difficulty with this sand and he said, "Yes, pine needles fall in it, and it's a very expensive sand, and it has to be protected, and it's a chore to get all the pine needles out of the sand, I asked him, "Well, could you put a tarpaulin over it?"

He said yes.

I said, "Couldn't you hold the tarpaulin down with CBS blocks on the side?"

He said yes.

I said, "Don't you think that would keep a little boy out of the sand pile?" And, unbelievably he said yes.

Result: Three-million dollar verdict.

Was that luck? I don't know.

All of these cases, Holl, Knapp and Kaylor, were given a world of publicity and I was a busy person.

I tried the Little John case in Key West, involving a brain-damaged boy, for three weeks. A 1.5 million-dollar jury verdict there, the first million-dollar verdict in Key West.

It was a very serious case, and the little baby would need care for the rest of his life. I took a team with me: an associate, an investigator and a secretary. We stayed at one of the lovely resorts in Key West, and the first day went very well. We got a good jury.

That evening, I was in my room, and there was a knock on the door.

I asked, "Who's there?" And someone said, "Turndown lady." I didn't know what turndown lady meant.

I opened the door to a very attractive young woman, who said she had come to turn down the sheets. She asked me what we were doing in Key West. I told her I was trying a malpractice case in the state Court. She said, "Well, my daddy's on that jury, and he said you had a good day."

Well, I didn't pursue that any further, but she continued to make comments for the next three weeks.

This was a huge trial. We had witnesses flying in from all over the country, and on the weekends, we would charter a huge sailboat and take everybody out and try to relax.

The jury was out for hours, and you could hear them deliberating, shouting at each other. I would walk over and put my ear to the jury door and listen and be upset by some of the jurors arguing that a huge verdict would make their insurance rates go up. It went on and on.

The judge would come out from time to time and quietly put his ear to the door as well to hear what was going on.

Finally, we got a verdict at 2:00 o'clock in the morning. We had all been waiting patiently across the street in a local bar and, to be frank, I think I had too much to drink. I was worn to a frazzle.

The jury came in with a verdict and handed it to the judge. It was published, and the judge excused the jury.

I did something then that was stupid indeed. As the jury started to file out of the jury box I stood up and said, "I'm very sorry, we cannot accept this verdict, it's too cheap."

The judge shook his head and said we would discuss it tomorrow. That was a blunder, very poor behavior, and the next day the judge didn't say anything about it and we went on and got it behind us.

In all of the years that I have practiced law, I have never been held in contempt. I have had several judges caution me, which is only natural.

The Navy awarded me six medals for my time in the service and one of them is a "Good Conduct" medal which simply means that in my Naval career I was never in trouble, never reprimanded and never, in effect, disobeyed the rules.

Key West brings back many, many memories for me. I don't mean to suggest that I've been a Mr. Goody-Two-Shoes, because I had some small problems of misconduct.

When I was in high school in Tallahassee a friend of mine and I were shooting squirrels in the downtown cemetery from huge oak trees. He had his car parked there, and he had a 22 rifle. Someone called the police, but we saw them coming and we put the rifle in the back of the car with the squirrels that we had shot and just stood there.

The police asked us what we were doing, and two teenage boys simply said, "Nothing."

Well at that point, one squirrel we had shot was hanging apparently by one paw in the oak tree. The squirrel fell at the foot of the police officer and he said, "Ah-ha."

Well, he took us to the Tallahassee Police Station and put the two of us in jail for several hours, but we got a firm lecture, and I do remember the squirrel event.

Another one a little more serious involved a beautiful blonde secretary and me going to Sebring to watch the automobile races.

We had had too much liquor in the car and we were sitting out there in the sun watching the cars go by my Cadillac convertible, she in her bikini, me in my swim trunks, both of us bare headed with too much sun and too much champagne.

Upon leaving Sebring Racetrack that afternoon an old gentlemen in front of me was driving entirely too slow so I would bump him to nudge him along. Finally, I got him out of the way and got out on the highway and all of a sudden there's a police car behind with its lights flashing and so on.

He pulled us over and he could tell that we were in bad shape. He put me in the back of the police car but I got out on the other side and I ran around and around the police car with the police officer chasing me.

Finally, he got the two of us in the police car and took us to the police station and put us in jail. She was in a cell adjoining mine. I made a fool out of myself. I screamed over and over again that I was a lawyer and that I had a Constitutional right to make a phone call and on, and on.

My friend was crying in the next cell asking me, "J. B., what can I tell my boyfriend?"

Finally, a short deputy came to the cell, and he said, "Mr. Spence, how can I help you?"

I told him that I wanted to exercise my Constitutional rights to call a lawyer. He said sure. He unlocked the cell and said, "Follow me."

As we went down the corridor, he suddenly gave me a big nudge and pushed me into a padded cell. Then he got a firehose and nearly drowned me in the padded cell, and I quit talking.

We were released the next day and came back to Miami and went our separate ways, but I had to go back to Sebring for a Traffic Court hearing.

I lost my driver's license for a year, but I did have the good sense to walk around to apologize to everyone that I had insulted and give them a serious apology.

We didn't win them all. I went to Atlanta, Georgia, and tried a brain-damage case for three weeks and lost. Flying home alone, I went over that entire trial in my mind, thinking, "What could I have done better?"

I had the same feeling after a three-week trial in New Orleans, an anesthesia death case. I lost that one also. But the absolute, totally, completely worst loss in my life was in Orlando, Florida.

I represented a young woman who was a patient of an Orlando psychiatrist. She had previously tried to commit suicide. She had heard voices; she wanted to be hospitalized. Her doctor left town, and on the weekend, she climbed a tree, poured lighter fluid all over herself, and set herself on fire. Horrible injuries.

After a three-week trial in Orlando, the jury rendered a verdict for the plaintiff for two million dollars. Then incredible things happened: The trial judge took the verdict away, dismissed our case, and threw us out of Court. I couldn't believe it.

We took an appeal, and the District Court agreed with the trial judge. We took an appeal to the Supreme Court, and the Supreme Court said on a technical basis they wouldn't hear the case, but two justices on the Florida Supreme Court said that the lower Courts were clearly in error.

When the Court uses the word "error," they are politely telling the lower Court, "You have ignored substantial evidence in the record and in effect swept it under the rug and given the verdict to the physician."

In all my years of practicing law, this is the only case that I can point to where my client was, in my opinion, judicially raped. I have very bitter feelings about this case. It was a gross miscarriage of justice. I was at a loss about what to do.

Of course, we took an appeal, but I also decided I would try to analyze what the trial judge had done.

The trial judge in Orlando was known as "Crazy Joe" Baker. Throughout my three-week trial, the local attorneys would speak to me in the hall at the courthouse or in the elevator or on the street and ask me, "How's 'Crazy Joe' treating you? Watch out, be careful, keep up your guard."

Local attorneys told me that when divorce cases were being heard by "Crazy Joe," he would suggest that the woman meet him that evening for a drink. A litigant before the judge, having a drink with the judge!

I personally saw him standing in the hall holding the hand of a very attractive female juror serving on another case. She was trying to get her hand free from the judge's grip. He wouldn't let her go.

I could overhear him saying, "Have we not met before? I'm a Circuit Court judge. I wish you were in my courtroom."

"Crazy Joe" told me he was receiving a barrage of phone calls from the local doctors concerning my malpractice trial.

I thought about all of this information and I was torn between two rules: One, my Constitutional right to criticize, and, two, my duty to uphold the dignity of the judiciary.

I think I would have been some kind of moral coward to hide his reprehensible conduct. I also knew that I had a specific duty under the Florida Bar rules to report judicial misbehavior, and I did so without hesitation or regret.

I find the comments of Supreme Court Justice Frankfurter helpful in this matter. "Judges as persons or courts as an institution are entitled to no greater immunity from criticism than other persons or institutions. Just because the holders of judicial office are identified with the interest of justice, they may not forget their common human frailties and fallibilities.

"Sometimes there have been martinets upon the bench as there have also been pompous wielders of authority who have used the paraphernalia of power in support of what they called their dignity. Therefore, judges must be kept mindful of their limitations and their ultimate public responsibility by a vigorous stream of criticism expressed with candor, however blunt."

Several lawyers told me that in their opinion, "Crazy Joe" was a disgrace to the judiciary.

I have filed complaints involving other judges, and I can assure you that you pay a price for honoring this duty. Nasty comments are made, and you get cold, angry stares. So be it.

After filing my complaint concerning "Crazy Joe" Baker with the Judicial Qualifications Commission, the procedure was that I had to give a deposition, my sworn testimony of what I thought had occurred.

"Crazy Joe" Baker came to Miami on one Saturday, a Florida Bar Grievance Committee lawyer attended, and my deposition was taken.

"Crazy Joe" asked me what my problem was with him, and I told him eyeball-to-eyeball sitting about five feet apart the following: I said, "First of all, you are a disgrace to the Bar. Secondly, you have absolutely no business being a Circuit Court judge, and your reputation in this community is in the gutter. Everyone knows that you've been trying to date women seeking a divorce before you, and you're asking them to meet you at a bar for a drink."

I simply wanted the Florida Bar, through the Judicial Qualifications Commission, to take him off the bench because he was in my opinion a dishonest judge.

An example is the fact that he rode home with a juror in my case, a juror sitting in on my trial, and he would meet with the jurors alone in the jury room. And heaven knows what he told them.

But on top of all of that, an alternate juror had gone out to the jury foreman's car and put a note on his windshield, "Don't give her anything. She settled with her father's insurance company."

The jury foreman showed this note to Judge Baker and assured the judge that the note would not influence him in any way, and that the jury had already decided the issue of liability and were simply discussing the amount of money.

Notwithstanding that statement from the foreman, Judge Baker stated that he didn't believe him, and that he, Judge Baker, thought that the note on the windshield had decided the case.

In other words, the judge simply brushed aside the sworn testimony of the foreman of the jury because of his anxiety to defeat this woman's legitimate claim.

I would like to take you back a moment and show you in black and white the gross miscarriage of justice in this case.

The Paddock case was appealed to the Supreme Court and the Supreme Court was asked to grant a new trial. The majority opinion held that the Supreme Court did not have jurisdiction on an extremely technical basis in that the Paddock case did not conflict with any other case on the same points; however, two dissenting judges, Justice Barkett and Justice Kogan, said the following at 553 So. Reporter 2d Series, Page 168: Linda K. Paddock, Petitioner, vs. Chawallur de Vassy Chacko, M.D., Respondent.

"There's no question that Florida law recognizes that physicians owe their patients a duty to exercise reasonable and ordinary care. The breach of that duty in a medical malpractice case is established by proving that a practitioner has departed from the accepted standards of care recognized as reasonable and prudent by similar healthcare providers.

"Elsewhere the Court has held that there is a strong public policy in this state to leave questions of the foreseeability of damages with the jury when reasonable people may differ.

"Paddock is no more than a simple medical malpractice case to which Wale applies. The question follows whether the defendant physician has conformed to or departed from reasonable standards of psychiatric care in discharging his duty as Paddock's physician.

"The patient alleged that her physician departed from the applicable standard of care by failing to recognize the seriousness of her illness, by failing to properly prescribe medications to control her illness and by failing to properly advise or treat her when she telephoned for emergency assistance.

"In a telephone conversation, Dr. Chacko recommended hospitalization. Paddock testified that she did, in fact, agree to hospitalization whereas Dr. Chacko testified Paddock refused.

"Although there was testimony on both sides of this issue, the District Court ignored the factual dispute and found that the patient's refusal to be hospitalized was an 'admitted fact.'

"Because of the erroneous finding, the District Court framed the issue as to whether the psychiatrist had a duty to involuntarily hospitalize a seriously disturbed patient after the patient refused to heed the doctor's advice to hospitalize herself.

"It's very difficult to ignore Paddock's meritorious argument that the District Court misapplied the principles enumerated in Wale and other cases establishing the applicable duty of care, thus I would grant jurisdiction on the basis of Wale."

In my opinion, Linda Paddock was judicially raped and suffered a gross miscarriage of justice.

I represented a railroad worker who was doing some repairs on the rails, when he had to relieve himself. There was no portable potty around, so he went out in the woods and squatted down. A rattlesnake bit him in the butt.

We tried this case in the Dade County Circuit Court, and I went down to the Serpentarium in South Miami and rented a huge, live diamondback rattlesnake and brought him in a big glass case to the courthouse, but the judge wouldn't let the snake come in the courtroom.

He did let the jury go out in the lobby to see the rattlesnake. We won.

I kept getting publicity, which I enjoyed because it was all favorable: victories, victories, victories.

The *Wall Street Journal* had one of their reporters come to Miami and spend several days with me, and they published the story of my life with my photograph on the front page.

The morning the paper was delivered at the local newsstand, I bought all 20 copies. The newsman wanted to know why I was doing that, and I showed him one and said, "I can't help but be proud of having my life story told and my picture on the front page of the *Wall Street Journal*." That was a high moment for me.

I have spoken many places about the complicated subject of medical malpractice, trying to explain that there are many issues involved.

Recently, I spoke at the Medical School at the University of Miami, and the students booed me off the stage.

I also spoke at one of the local hospitals, and they gave me a Marine Corps flack helmet to wear. One of the doctors sent a note up to the host saying, "Who invited the devil?"

On another occasion, I spoke at a largely Latin hospital and was called a communist. I had to get a security guard to walk me to my car. I've been insulted at social events and received my share of hate mail.

Suing doctors and hospitals is not a popular area of the law. On some occasions, I've been quoted, "I enjoy suing the bastards."

I've seen some very dishonest and unethical things in this area of the law: Doctors changing their records, doctors destroying their records and rewriting them, nurses changing their records, gross lies, distortions, and hardball lawsuits.

It's nice to win, but the victory is a great deal more than the lawyer victory. I'm representing people who have lost their child or a husband who's lost his wife, or a young woman who's lost her leg, or a baby who's blinded, or relatives of people who were killed in an air crash or at a railroad crossing or in a car explosion.

Everyone who comes to my office brings a tragedy, and they're all little people; they don't have 50,000 dollars to finance a case.

I get so personally and emotionally involved with the people that I represent. I don't call them clients. They're people with serious problems, and they want their day in Court in front of an honest judge and a fair jury. My role is to help them accomplish that and hopefully to get them appropriate financial relief.

Take the Holl case, for example. This young woman's life was destroyed through the negligence of the hospital's nurses and the doctors. To keep her alive would cost a fortune.

My job is to try my best to see that these folks get the relief they're entitled to. Practicing this kind of law can be stressful.

One of the worst scenes of all is when the jury knocks on the door and the bailiff speaks to the jury and tells the judge that the jury has reached a verdict. The judge tells the bailiff, "Bring the jury in," and the jury walks in not looking at anyone. Sometimes, their eyes are downcast. They slowly take their seats in the jury box.

The judge asks, "Have you reached a verdict?"

The foreman stands up and says, "Yes, sir." The foreman hands the verdict to the bailiff, the bailiff walks across the courtroom to the judge. Speed? About a mile an hour, an eternity.

The bailiff hands the verdict to the judge; the judge reads it expressionless, hands it back to the bailiff. The bailiff, once more at a snail's pace, walks the verdict back to the foreman.

Now the judge says, "Publish the verdict," and an eternity goes by before the foreman speaks. My heart races; I can't get my breath; 1.8 million-dollar verdict.

When the Knapp verdict was rendered, I fainted and fell on the floor. This is part of the thrill, the challenge, the ecstasy and the pain of being a trial lawyer in this kind of litigation. I'll do it until the day I die, I hope.

I recently handled a blind baby case, retrolental fibroplasia, a premature child overdosed with oxygen, blinded for life.

In another case, a doctor's wife went into the hospital for a simple D & C. The endotracheal tube was placed in her esophagus rather than her trachea. Her stomach blew up like an airplane tire. She was deprived of oxygen, brain-damaged, and she passed away, leaving a husband and four minor children.

My client went to the hospital with a pistol looking for the anesthesiologist and would have killed him if he found him. And when I told the jury that story, they all nodded their head in agreement.

A number of young men have been killed by the railroad while fishing on a railroad trestle. The former chief investigator for the railroad asked the president of the railroad what should be done about the death of these young men, and the president responded, "Kill the little bastards."

During the railroad trestle case involving two boys fishing from the trestle, I called as a witness the surviving boy, age 12. I had met with him and his mother in person. I had shown him the photographs of the scene and asked him if he would testify concerning how the accident occurred, where he was standing, and where the other boy was when he was struck by the train and killed, one of the "little bastards" as defined by the president of the railroad.

I only asked a few questions, and it was apparent that he was both nervous and frightened. When the railroad lawyers started to cross-examine him, he became more frightened.

The railroad lawyer asked him if he had been promised a ride on Mr. Spence's "big boat." The little boy, now teary-eyed, replied yes.

I was stunned, and I stood there in dismay. I could not believe what I was hearing, a little boy telling the jury that I had, in effect, bribed him with the promise to ride on my big boat.

All of my credibility was on the line.

I was at a loss as to what to do. I glanced back at the people in the courtroom and saw the boy's mother. I called her to the stand, and she quickly told the jury that I had been perfectly polite with her and her son, and that I had made no promise of any kind or any thing.

Think where I would be in the eyes of the jury if his mother was not present and able to testify. The railroad lawyer simply invented this dirty trick…dishonest and unethical. We won the case.

I kept a file during the case called dirty tricks, and I saved them to destroy the defense lawyer's credibility. Thankfully, we do not see a great deal of this frequently. Dishonesty and deceit rarely win.

The railroad had the dirtiest litigation team I had ever seen. Over the last eight years, railroads have broken federal rules by failing to promptly report hundreds of fatal accidents; 71 of them in this last year [July 11—12 *New York Times*—RR Articles].

Important evidence is routinely destroyed or lost. Defective signal equipment is routinely corrected quickly before an independent investigation.

On average, one person a day dies at a crossing in the United States. Federal judges have routinely sanctioned the railroads for their total dishonesty.

On one occasion I represented a woman whose shoe was caught in the wide tread on an escalator in a downtown Miami department store. I sued the department store and won the case.

Some time later, I represented the parent of a little girl who fell on this same escalator because of the wide tread and had four of her little fingers cut off.

Once more, I sued the department store and learned that following the first lawsuit, the department store's insurance company had requested that the escalators be brought up to date with new narrow tread that would prevent customers from being injured.

The department store refused to do that, and when this was presented to the jury, they compensated the little girl for losing her fingers and they added punitive damages to try to encourage the department store to put safety first.

Some time later, I was in this department store to have lunch, and I observed that all of the escalators were closed down and being repaired. The new tread escalator was being installed. I stood there in that store thinking that I was the only person there who knew why we were getting new safety escalators. It was a moment of pride.

I think that law schools don't train lawyers to be trial lawyers. The only way in my view that you can become a trial lawyer is the hard way, the school of hard knocks, losing, losing, losing.

I think Babe Ruth had the record for the most home runs and the most strike outs, but he was in the game.

My thoughts or my formula for winning a lawsuit are pretty simple. They are as follows:

1. Know every fact in the case; visit the scene, the operating room, ride in the train engine, operate the machine, have total knowledge of all of the facts;

2. Know the law. Prepare memos for the key points, review all pertinent cases, good and bad. Think;

3. Know the witnesses, analyze them, their background, education, occupation. Establish a rapport with the witnesses;

4. Your personal attitude: You are well-prepared, you are polite, you are calm, you are respectful and you have honest humility.

Recently I was in Texas speaking to the Texas Bar Association young lawyers' section, and there were four of us on the program on the stage at the same time. Each of us had practiced law for over 40 years, and each of us in different words said the same thing: Credibility, credibility, credibility.

You simply have to earn the trust of the jury. That's easy to say, and a lot of young lawyers won't accept it. They want to use Rambo tactics like you see in the movies or on TV, and, in my view, that won't work.

I pretend I'm a guide in the trial, calmly pointing the way to a fair verdict. I try to be calm, confident and modest, plain-speaking, respectful to everyone.

I also review my "blunders file" to alert myself to the costly errors I made in the past.

I think of all of the lawyers in the old Nichols firm, I lost the most cases, but I went on to have considerable success. I also have a frame of mind that my partners used to tease me about.

I simply think if I do my job, the defense doesn't have a chance. But I continue to make mistakes.

Recently I represented an African American couple who lost their only daughter in a railroad crossing collision. The unbelievable occurred. At the end of the day, we had a jury of six African Americans. Never happened to me before in my life; it just happened. But leaving the courthouse and walking back to my office with the railroad lawyer who was in the same building, I said too much.

I told my friend that when this lawsuit was over, I would own the railroad and that I would get a boxcar verdict, and he didn't have a chance. Braggadocio!

The next morning when we went to the courthouse, the railroad lawyer wasn't there. A young associate was present and he told the judge that the senior partner was home and had been up all night with a serious case of diarrhea. Ha! The judge declared a mistrial. My six African American jurors walked out the door, and I paid a big price for my bragging.

We got a new trial date and on the way to the courthouse that morning, I stopped at a drugstore and I bought about 50 dollars' worth of junk medicine: hemorrhoid medicine, Alka Seltzer, aspirin; an armload. I put it in a big brown bag and set it on the defense table.

My friend came in, a Harvard graduate, and inquired: "What's this?"

I told him, "If you get a pain or an ache in any part of your body, you reach in there and cure it because I'm not going to let you get away with that phony diarrhea excuse, old friend."

The lawsuits went on. I tried a case with the president of the Florida

Bar in Jacksonville, a very fine defense lawyer. It was a Volkmann's contracture case.

A boy had broken his arm. The doctor put the cast on too tight, it cut off the circulation in the child's arm, and the boy lost his arm.

This was a two-week trial, a very close question on liability because there was a huge conflict between what the mother had to say and what the doctor had to say about phone calls.

I sensed we were in trouble. The jury came in and asked a question of the judge. None of the jurors would look at my client or me.

When the jury returned to deliberate, I begged the client to let me settle the case, and she wouldn't do it. I kept pleading with her that I had a sense we were in trouble.

Finally, she said okay. I walked over to the defense attorney and accepted his offer, we shook hands, and I turned to the judge and told him the case had been settled.

As that happened, there was a knock on the door. The jury had reached a verdict. The judge turned, took the verdict, turned it face down, thanked the jury for their service and excused them.

The judge said, "Mr. Spence, would you like to see this verdict?

I said, "No, sir."

In my mind I didn't want there to be a half-a-million dollar jury verdict there and I had settled for much, much less.

Then the judge asked the defense lawyer if he would like to see the verdict. He said no. Then he paused a little bit and he said, "Yes, I do want to see it."

The judge turned it over and showed it to both of us. It was a verdict for the defense. I felt like Robin Hood. I caught a plane and came home pleased.

One more trial. Tom Rumberger was a very young Circuit Court judge in Melbourne, Florida, and when he decided that he would rather go back to practicing law, he opened a fine defense firm. He and I had one trial.

Just for the fun of it, I proposed that neither one of us would make a single objection for the entire length of the trial. We shook hands on it.

We picked a jury the first day, made opening statements; no

objections. Went through the second day; no objections. The third day, the judge called us to the bench and said, "Is there something I should know?" And we, with straight faces, said, "No, sir."

The fourth day, no objections. The judge laughingly joked and said, "Can I stay home tomorrow?"

We went through all of the final argument, the whole nine yards. Neither one of us made one objection.

I still rarely make objections; only when I think I'm hurt. Many times a lawyer with me will almost pull my coat off urging me to object.

People ask me why I'm successful in the courtroom. I've had lawyers watch me for a day and tell a friend they didn't think that I do a very good job, that I seem too quiet, too modest, and not very aggressive.

I think I have that style because of my life dealing with people: the paper routes, driving a laundry truck, being a waiter, bagging groceries, cutting lawns, being a mailman. I think of my life experiences with ordinary people give me some humility and common sense. It has been a wonderful trip, and life has been very good to me.

We had a case that involved me going to Cuba. I think it was Batista time. We represented some people who signed up for a tour package in Miami, but while they were in Havana, they were in a terrible automobile accident because of the tour driver's negligence.

I went to Havana to take some depositions and investigate the matter. My investigator went ahead of me. He met me at the plane with a limousine, a box of terrific Cuban cigars, and we checked into the Nationale Hotel. We had dinner at the Floridita Restaurant.

My investigator got arrested for taking photographs at the scene without a permit, and I had to do some legal maneuvers to get him out of jail.

We went to the Tropicana nightclub. All of the beautiful, long-legged Cuban women were dancing on the stage and I joined them.

When we went back to Miami, my boss asked me if I had had a good time. I thought I had lost my job because we spent a lot of money in Havana.

He told me, "J. B., you only go down this road once. Have some fun."

You never quit learning if you practice trial law. The seasons shift, the jurors change, the judges change, the law changes, your enemies grow stronger and there's a constant battle.

The learning part is wonderful. Trial lawyers in my mind are unique, both criminal and civil trial lawyers.

I taught at a trial lawyers' seminar at Harvard University, which made me quite proud, and I bragged about it a good bit. We were teaching young lawyers from across America courtroom skills, and the faculty was made up of unique people: An anthropologist who talked to gorillas, a movie producer, a TV director, authors of books, famous speakers, a very challenging, somewhat intimidating group because you learned a lot you didn't know.

I've tried to pass this on.

I taught at the University of Miami Law School to seniors, trial tactics. I've written a book, "Final Argument."

I treasure my memory of Congressman Dante Fascell taking me to the United States Supreme Court and hearing Chief Justice Warren say, "Mr. Spence, welcome to the Supreme Court."

I stood there in awe, the farm boy, the Navy mess cook, the truck driver…only in America.

There is an award given every year to a lawyer chosen by the Academy of Florida Trial Lawyers. It's the Perry Nichols Award. It has been given in the past to a governor, a congressman, Supreme Court justices, and one year it was awarded to me. It was an extremely proud moment and something I will cherish forever.

There's not a day that goes by that I don't look at the big photograph on the wall of my mentor, my friend, and my almost father, Perry Nichols.

We had a lawyer in Miami that none of us could beat. His name is Bill Hoeveler. He is currently sitting on the Federal District Court in Miami. He's very tall, very handsome and sophisticated, but a most modest trial lawyer.

He wore seersucker suits. His briefcase looked like it was about 100 years old, and when he sat it down, it would collapse. He had an extraordinary way with jurors. Women loved him.

I hated to try cases against him. I looked up all the information about him, trying to get a handle on how not to be defeated by him every time. He was, when I tried cases against him, with a big defense firm so a number of us trial lawyers hatched a plot.

We asked the two United States senators from Florida to appoint Bill Hoeveler to the federal bench and after some discussion, they agreed. Or course, he was a topnotch candidate, a real gentleman and excellent lawyer, and a man of great depth. His rating today in the judicial polls is number one.

I was president of the Dade County Bar at the time of his investiture, and he invited me to participate in that program. I was the last speaker. I told the story about the plot, our game plan to take him off of Flagler, out of the Dade County Courthouse, and put him someplace where he couldn't continue to beat us.

At the end of my story I turned and looked at Bill Hoeveler and said, "Bye, bye, Bill."

Those solemn, serious federal judges sitting there found no humor in that at all.

I think my heroes are in this order: Perry Nichols, President Lincoln, President Truman, and both of the President Roosevelts, Theodore and Franklin.

I have a whole library on Lincoln. I have read about him at great length from his birth to his death, his losing his mother, his having a father who didn't care for him at all, all of the failures, all of the disappointments, and all of the challenges.

And also the others, Truman and the Roosevelts. I think of these folks every day. They encourage me every day.

I must be one of those people who truly loves the law, but I don't necessarily mean the printed law or the statutes and all that. I think my passion is in the drama, the challenge of representing poor people against the giants, the corporate giants, big business. This is a challenge that I feel every day after many years of practicing law.

I'm still in the office every day. I have a busy caseload. All of them are interesting and challenging cases.

One of our law clerks did a search the other day for all of the appellate opinions that our firm has had where my name appears. The first one was in 1953. I lost.

We've handled a total of 268 appeals. Many of those decisions are landmark cases, new laws, frontiers, and many of them were earned the hard way.

At my age, I decided to join the AARP in Coral Gables. There are about 100 members, and the AARP has designated me as one of their approved counsel. I get phone calls night and day from these folks: They need someone to draw a will or handle a traffic matter. They're wonderful people, and they're doing a great job, and I'm proud to be part of them. Many of the things that they would like done for them, I'm not qualified to do, but I help them get help.

The AARP is one of the most powerful groups of people in America. They stand for a lot of great ideals and they fight very hard for the elderly.

I recently read a book, *Age Power*, about how life expectancy has increased and how really the backbone of America are the elderly.

Another venture for me was becoming an Ombudsman. This is a program approved by the federal government and the Florida government. It involves being a detective, really, a helper for people in nursing homes and assisted living facilities.

You actually have to go to school to be an Ombudsman. You walk through all the Florida statutes and federal statutes and other rules and regulations that apply to nursing homes and, in addition to that, you visit nursing homes with a supervisor and learn how to conduct an investigation.

It's a serious matter. I did that, and the Governor of Florida appointed me to serve as an Ombudsman. My duties are to respond to complaints, to go to the nursing home and try to solve the complaint by writing up what I find.

Some of these nursing homes are horrible places. Patients are neglected, they lie in urine-soaked beds for days, they have pressure sores, they are overmedicated, they are treated very poorly; they are left to wander in the street. The horror stories about nursing homes are terrible, pathetic and sad.

These activities with AARP, being an Ombudsman and the practice of law keep me busy. After the Governor appointed me an Ombudsman, the nursing home industry in Florida had a fit. They wrote Governor

Bush a long letter, a hate letter really, about my appointment.

They view me as an enemy of their business and accuse me of being an Ombudsman so I can get nursing home cases. Every adverse newspaper story about me and my life was also sent to the Governor. There was a big write-up in the *Wall Street Journal* about this and in the Miami paper also.

The Governor passed the matter on to the State Attorney General. He reviewed the matter and rendered an opinion on my behalf, stating that I have every right to be an Ombudsman.

I am proud to have so many enemies from that field. I love it.

Most people have no knowledge at all about the battle behind the scenes to keep the courthouse door open. The people I represent are little people. They have no money. They can't write a check for 25,000 dollars for me to take the case.

I take the case on a contingency basis. If we win, if we are successful with a settlement or a trial, under the Supreme Court-approved contingency fee contract, I am paid. If I invest 25,000 dollars, 50,000 dollars or 100,000 dollars in a case and months of my life and lose it, I don't get paid.

This discussion about frivolous lawsuits simply isn't true. If I handled frivolous lawsuits, I would have to close the front door.

There is a massive effort across America: think tanks, Chambers of Commerce, tort reform organizations, defense organizations, huge ads in the *Wall Street Journal*, on television, on and on, designed to protect corporate America and punish the little man and close down the courthouse…vicious, cruel, mean, greedy, selfish.

Recently, the Ohio Legislature passed a so-called tort reform bill about 150 pages long that practically closed the courthouse door to innocent victims of negligence.

The trial lawyers in that state filed a lawsuit against the State of Ohio which wound up in the Ohio Supreme Court, the issue being whether the Ohio tort law was constitutional or not.

Four of the seven members of the Ohio Supreme Court voted and wrote a lengthy opinion, holding in essence that the Ohio Legislature had violated the citizens of Ohio's Constitutional rights.

Of course, the business interests in Ohio, Chambers of Commerce, corporations and others are hysterical over this because it affects their pocketbook.

The word today is that that group is gathering a massive sum of money and have plans to replace the four Supreme Court Justices who voted against the Legislature, so the bet is on. All four of the Ohio Supreme Court Justices are up for reelection and the game plan is to take them off the Court and replace them with business interest judges.

Some of the current candidates for president are basically saying the same thing, and the idea was also floated here in Florida that the liberal members of the Florida Supreme Court would be replaced by pro-business candidates.

It is a vicious fight across the nation, and we trial lawyers have a battle on our hands.

Let me quote from a letter from the president of Associated Industries of Florida, the voice of Florida business, sent to the incoming president of the American Bar Association.

He says, "I firmly believe that the very existence of our Constitutional protection and way of life depends on attorneys more than any other group, including the armed forces.

"On the other hand, the vast majority of very distinguished attorneys throughout this nation have allowed a small group, which I affectionately call 'the scum bags,' take over the legal profession and the view of the public.

"I speak of the trial lawyers and their unethical, un-American and illegal activities. We all know who they are and what they do."

He continues, "The fat cat, scumbag trial lawyers violate every rule, law and ethical standard and get away with it. We must stand up and slam the 'Scumbags.'"

The author of this letter is John L. Shebel, who is the president and chief ethics officer at the Associated Industries of Florida. He copied all members of the Supreme Court of Florida, and, as I say, the battle is on.

At the moment, we trial lawyer "scumbags" are planning to file a lawsuit similar to the one that was filed in Ohio for the same purpose.

The last session of the Legislature passed horrible legislation affecting the rights of Florida citizens, capping damages, shortening the Statute of Limitations, and many others.

At a recent AMA meeting, there was a proposal that physicians not treat trial lawyers or their families. Where are we going?

They also want to cap lawyers' fees. They want me to work for 10 percent rather than the standard attorney's fee. One of the state senators from Jacksonville was on TV after the Legislation was passed, and he proudly bragged that it had been "payback" time by the Legislature in passing this legislation for all of the contributions big business had made to the members of the Legislature.

It's a vicious battle. We're going to sue the state, and we have the same team that has been successful in other states fighting this same battle.

Recently, Governor Bush said that he was opposed to a patient's right to sue if they had been negligently injured by an HMO. He said that the right to sue would be "an avenue of revenue for the trial lawyers."

In other words, if an HMO denies a member of your family needed and appropriate care and a member of your family dies as a result of that negligence, you have no legal remedy.

Is this America?

Does corporate America own America?

Have our Constitutional legal rights vanished?

These people are without shame. I am reminded of an event in the past. We had a state senator who was president of the Senate and his name for the trial lawyers was "bloodsuckers." It took us a little time but we got an excellent candidate and defeated Mr. Bloodsucker, but it wasn't easy.

If you knew the cruelty, the selfishness, the greed and dishonesty of corporate America, you would be in horror. Countless examples exist of circumstances in which corporations have abused the power of technology, raped the environment, and recklessly and even purposely, endangered many lives with untested, knowingly defective products, and in other ways sacrificed the interest of innocent victims on the altar of corporate profit.

Corporate evil would have gone undetected, undeterred and unpunished were it not for the vigilance of trial lawyers who undertook to do a job the government could not or would not do.

Understandably, big business' interests lack a social conscience and are willing to sacrifice safety concerns to maximize profits. They have worked very hard in the past and they will continue in the future.

We are all familiar with the Pinto car explosions, the defective gas tank, cars exploding and killing whole families, burning them alive. All the while, Ford knew of this defect and coldly calculated it would be cheaper to kill a number of people burning them alive than it was to recall the Pinto and correct the defect. Corporate murder. Another example is the Bronco defective roll-overs, death, disasters, with the manufacturer having full knowledge of a defect and putting profit ahead of safety. Consider also: The Dalcon Shield, an incredible disaster, a crime. Phen-Fen drugs, heart attacks, hundreds of deaths. The Bork Haley heart valves, fractured, defective. Hundreds have died.

Tobacco. We all saw the executives of the tobacco industry testify in front of Congress that they had no knowledge that tobacco would harm anyone. Lies, deceit, greed, profits, criminal behavior.

In today's issue of the *New York Times,* we have a report from the Institutes of Medicine, the medical arm of the Academy of Science. It was reported that approximately 98,000 deaths occur from medical errors every year in the United States.

An example: Betty Lehman, a 39-year-old health columnist for the *Boston Globe,* died after an overdose of chemotherapy for breast cancer.

Another case: Willie King had part of his wrong leg amputated. I had a case like that in Miami. A local surgeon amputated the wrong leg. We never went to trial. The case was settled for the insurance policy limits.

This is a shocking report from an unbiased group from the medical community. The list is endless: State Farm fraudulent auto repairs, breast implants.

Our firm handled several hundreds of them. I've seen the women. I know what they went through to have those implants leak silicone into their body.

Thalidomide, thousands of children born without arms or legs. One horror story after another all across America, and big business calls us scumbags?

I had a number of those Dalcon Shield cases. A young woman in Key West died as a consequence of the Dalcon Shield, leaving a husband and two small children. This case was settled without filing the suit because Dalcon Shield did not want their dishonesty revealed.

A. H. Robbins Company, a family-controlled pharmacological manufacturer, distributed over four million Dalcon Shields in 80 countries with false claims of efficiency and safety.

In the United States, more than two million women were fitted with these untested contraceptive devices by doctors who believed the misleading claims of the manufacturer. Thousands of women suffered serious damage caused by the shield, from pelvic infection to sterility, miscarriage and even death.

In this litigation, the Robbins' attorneys took depositions from the women, the victims, in which they asked not only intimate but demanding and even intimidating questions. We plaintiffs' layers call them "dirty questions."

For example, a wife was asked, "Prior to your marriage, did you have sexual relations with anybody other than your husband, and who were these sexual partners, their names?"

Another dirty question: Another victim was asked if she wore pantyhose and what fabric was used in the crotch.

Another dirty question: Robbins' attorneys asked another victim which way she wiped and how often and if she engaged in oral or anal sexual intercourse and, if so, how often. Once more, unbelievable, incredible corporate crime.

I have recently represented a number of young women students who were sexually assaulted on the campus of a local university. Each young woman was attacked by the insurance lawyers, with a demeaning approach, a trashing technique.

"Q. Who was your first boyfriend? Did you have sex? Give us the name of your second boyfriend. Did you have sex? What kind of sex?

"Have you ever smoked marijuana? Where and with whom and how often?

"Have you ever been arrested for anything? What was the reason?

"Did any of your boyfriends ever treat you violently? Provide us with a full copy of your medical records for your whole life," and on, and on, and on for hours.

That kind of defense lawyering makes me absolutely furious. I have to struggle to control my temper and sometimes I look at them and say, "Aren't you ashamed to practice law like that?"

The university security department was so grossly inadequate. At times, all of them left the campus.

Today we see a number of corporate crime trials taking place in America and some of them we see going to prison. It's about time.

We have big enemies, the Trial Bar does, and the innocent victims do.

President Bush, recently speaking to a gathering of doctors in Philadelphia, said, "These trial lawyers are blackmailers. They file all of these frivolous lawsuits. We have stupid jurors and lousy verdicts, and I'm going to change that."

Where would he take us?

Vice President Cheney calls us "terrorists."

We need to go back and examine our heritage and have a sound knowledge of our great heritage. It should be known by every educated citizen in America that the law is the foundation of our society.

I seriously doubt that law students today are taught about the Code of Hammurabi or when Moses brought the 10 Commandments down from Mount Sinai. And, of course, the Magna Carta forced upon John the Tyrant King at Runnymead on the River Thames June 15, 1215.

I would urge that this history and our Declaration of Independence and our Constitution be compulsory education in the 9th, 10th, 11th and 12th grades.

The Bill of Rights of 1791 and our Constitution established a right to trial by jury. That right is in jeopardy because corporate America owns America.

Are the American people prepared to rise above the smallness of selfishness of dogmatic self-satisfaction we see now, and get involved and face the problems of life in our society?

We lawyers have the obligation to lead and to teach and to overcome that smallness. The law is the rock that our nation has been built on.

My hope is that we think less about making money and more about our nation's future.

The Miami Herald | Editorial

Judicial independence under attack

The judge-bashing coming from critics of the judicial system was bad enough when it was confined to rhetoric from a noisy few on the outer fringes of the far right. Now, elected officials who wield power in Washington have made matters much worse. Led by U.S. Rep. Tom DeLay of Texas, the GOP majority leader, they are making deplorable comments of their own and trying to foment legislation designed to crush judicial independence.

Incensed that federal courts followed the law and the Constitution in rejecting Congress' virtual order to revisit the Terri Schiavo case, Rep. DeLay declared that "the time will come for the men responsible for this to answer for their behavior." Not to be outdone by the House Majority Leader, GOP Sen. John Cornyn of Texas suggested on the Senate floor that violence against judges might be motivated by frustration against perceived political decisions by judges.

This is reprehensible, irresponsible conduct by people who should know better. Rep. DeLay and his cohorts are sworn to uphold the Constitution, not undermine its most basic tenets. Yet they don't seem remotely familiar with the Constitution's demand for co-equal branches of government and a distinct separation of powers.

Earlier this month, Mr. DeLay said in a videotaped speech to a conference entitled "Confronting the Judicial War on Faith" that federal courts had "run amok" and that Congress had a duty to "reassert our constitutional authority over the courts." The chief of staff for Sen. Tom Coburn, Republican of Oklahoma, told the conference that "mass impeachment" might just be the only solution for the problem of judges who won't take orders from Congress.

At one point, Mr. DeLay himself came out in favor of impeachment. But when President Bush and Sen. Bill Frist, the majority leader in the upper chamber, both distanced themselves from these remarks, the Texas congressman appeared to back down—but only so much. In a class example of political double-talk, he said that he, too, believed in an "independent judiciary." Nevertheless, he insists that the Judiciary Committee investigate the Schiavo decisions to recommend possible legislation.

Rep. Steve King, R-Iowa, suggested another way to punish courts: "When their budget starts to dry up, we'll get their attention... If we're going to preserve our Constitution we must get them in line."

Get them in line? If this anti-judicial crusade is allowed to succeed, the Constitution itself will be trampled. Federal judges are nominated by the president and confirmed by the Senate for lifetime appointments. This ensures their independence and preserves our system of checks-and-balances. It distributes power to reduce the threat of tyranny. If Congress can dictate the outcome of lawsuits and trials, as it attempted to do in the Schiavo case, why have courts and judges? Rent a lobbyist instead.

The idea of Congress intervening in this way is a radical notion, just as preserving the integrity of the courts is a fundamentally conservative principle. President Franklin D. Roosevelt himself grew frustrated with the "nine old men" on the Supreme Court who blocked his liberal New Deal legislation in the 1930s. Congress balked at the court-packing scheme he devised as a way to control the court, and it proved to be his greatest domestic defeat. Today, the shoe is on the other foot as Mr. DeLay and his followers seek to intimidate the courts. Ever since Congress hurriedly approved the Terri Schiavo legislation, most Americans can see all too clearly which branch of government is running amok.

The Miami Herald | Editorial

Filibuster a hedge against majority stampede

For a brief moment last week it seemed that a compromise might be possible in the U.S. Senate to avert a nasty fight over the use of filibusters to block a vote on judicial candidates. It's been a custom in the Senate for nearly 200 years for the minority party to invoke filibusters and other anti-majority tactics, particularly when the other party controlled both the Senate and the presidency, which is the situation today. Although these practices commonly frustrate the majority, they have generally served the nation well as part of the system of checks and balances designed to protect the minority and promote compromise and consultation.

It was disappointing, therefore, to hear Senate Majority Leader Bill Frist, R-Tenn., turn down the offer of Democrats to allow a confirmation vote on four of seven stalled judicial nominations in return for doing away with the threat of changing the rules in order to quash filibusters. This brings the fight over judicial nominations to the brink of a partisan confrontation that is simply unnecessary.

Sen. Frist argues that he supports the principle that judicial nominees deserve an up-or-down vote. This is a simple enough proposition on its face, but it conveniently ignores the common use of delaying and blocking tactics in years past. During the 1990s, when power was divided between a GOP-controlled Senate and a Democratic White House, at least 20 appeals-court nominees were denied hearings by the Senate Judiciary Committee, for example. In other words, not only did the nominations not get to the floor of the Senate – they never even got the courtesy of a hearing. The only "principle" that seems to apply in this fight is whose ox is gored.

In years past, another check on the executive allowed senators to block action on nominees who happened to be from their state. This, too, may seem unfair, but it was a rule used by the Judiciary Committee beginning in 1995 that—conveniently—blocked three candidates to the Fourth U.S. Circuit Court of Appeals. In 2003, however, this rule was abolished. Anonymous floor "holds"—a particularly repugnant blocking technique—were also dropped.

This piece-by-piece dismantling of the checks-and-balances system certainly paves the way for more efficient government, but democracy wasn't designed to put efficiency above fairness or to stifle opposition. These protections are granted not to a party but to the American people, the ultimate beneficiaries of the checks and balances built into the U.S. system of government.

It is particularly unbecoming for Sen. Frist to say he does not support filibusters against judicial candidates. In 1999, he was part of a failed effort to block a vote on Richard Paez, a Ninth U.S. Circuit Court of Appeals nominee who finally was approved by the Senate four years after he was nominated. What kept Judge Paez from being blocked altogether was not the obedience to a principle against filibusters by his opponents but rather the fact that Sen. Frist and his colleagues didn't have the votes to make a filibuster effective.

As things stand, the courts are not "stacked" for one side or the other. It Democrats are forced to surrender the filibusters to stop judges they consider extreme, it turns the Senate into a rubber-stamp chamber. As the number of party-related appointments suggest, the attack on the filibuster rule isn't related to the partisan affiliation of active federal judges. More likely, it goes hand in hand with the assault on the federal judiciary by Rep. Tom DeLay, R-Tex., and his ardent supporters. It isn't enough to have their party appoint judges; the aim is to control the judges, and objective designed to undercut the independence of the judiciary in order to produce decisions that obey the extreme agenda of some GOP followers.

Based on polls following the approval of the Terri Schiavo law in Congress, it seems clear that most Americans understand that it's not for the Congress—or the president—to tell the courts how to decide cases. They understand that the rights of the political minority in the Senate, regardless of party, shouldn't be trampled in order to gain a temporary advantage. The best way to get things done in Congress is through consultation and compromise. Institutionalizing silence isn't.

I am deeply concerned by Republican efforts to undermine the rule of law by stripping the Senate of its right to extend debate over judicial nominations and by engaging in outright threats and intimidation against federal judges with whose decisions they disagree. Even after a judge was murdered in his Atlanta courtroom and the husband and mother of a federal judge were murdered in Chicago, the Republican leader of the House of Representatives responded to rulings in the Terri Schiavo case, by saying ominously: *"The time will come for the men responsible for this to pay for their behavior."*

Representative DeLay claimed his words had been chosen badly but, in the next breath, issued new threats against the same courts: *"We set up the courts. We have the power of the purse."* The chief of staff for a Republican senator called for "mass impeachment" under the bizarre theory that the President can declare any judge is no longer exhibiting "good behavior." The leader of one such group, the Family Research Council, recently said, *"There's more than one way to skin a cat, and there's more than one way to take a black robe off the bench."*

Another influential leader, James Dobson, added, *"The Congress can simply disenfranchise a court. They don't have to fire anybody or impeach them or go through that battle. All they have to do is say the 9th Circuit doesn't exist anymore, and it's gone."* In pursing the elimination of the filibuster, these extremists are seeking to undermine the deliberative character of our democracy because it stands in the way of their quest for absolute power. Their goal: an all-powerful executive using a weakened legislature to fashion a complaint judiciary in its own image. Maintaining the independence of the judiciary makes it possible for judges to protect and enforce individual rights, even when doing so is contrary to popular opinion and for the judicial branch to carry out its role in the system of checks and balances so artfully devised by our nation's founders. To be independent, the judiciary must be free of intimidation and manipulation from the legislative and executive branches. Congress and the courts must interact with respect, restraint and common purpose. Respect among these co-equal branches of government is vital. As Alexander Hamilton wrote, *"The independence of the judges is…requisite to guard the Constitution and the rights of individuals."*

WALL STREET JOURNAL

Doctors' Nemesis
Florida Lawyer Wings Big Malpractice Suits, and Loves Doing It

Folksy J.B. Spence Wastes No Mercy on Physicians,
Insurance Crisis or Not

Stripping a Plaintiff in Court
By KEN SLOCUM Staff Reporter

MIAMI—For weeks, the jury watched and listened in fascination, consumed by an unfolding tale of love, tragedy, and pursuit of revenge.

There was the young husband waiting in a hospital as his beautiful wife underwent minor surgery in a room but a few feet away. The dreaded emergency call "code blue,"—a medical situation gone awry. The husband's rush to a wife who would linger in a coma for nearly a year.

In heavy, accusing tones, the plaintiff's attorney, a folksy man with time etched in his creased features and whitened hair, declared that this woman was killed by "sloppy, incompetent medical care." The hospital and a doctor, and anesthesiologist, suffocated her brain and stilled her heart, he contended, allegedly by accidentally inserting an anesthesia tube into her stomach instead of her lungs. He boldly brought out—then brushed aside—the anguished husband's admission that he had stalked the hospital corridors with a gun in search of the anesthesiologist and revenge. And he showed the jury a videotape of what four children saw when they visited their comatose mother.

Verdict: $4.1 million against Miami's Cedars of Lebanon Hospital and the anesthesiologist.

"I enjoy suing the bastards," he says, succinctly revealing his motivation and his view of doctors.

Cap on Awards Proposed
Florida's legislature is expected to wrestle with the problem in a special

session next month. Almost every law being advanced will include some form of cap on medical-malpractice jury awards.

To Mr. Spence, that not only hurts the victim but also ignores the main culprit. "The leading cause of the problem is the bad doctor; there's a lot of sloppy medicine practiced in this state," he says. He advocates cracking down on poor medical practices and demanding regular testing and updating of physicians. "Hold their feet to the fire, and malpractice would be stopped in its tracks," he declares.

When Mr. Spence is involved, the likelihood of a big claim and big settlement is high. The average medical-malpractice attorney never wins a million-dollar verdict, but Mr. Spence has had 25, with eight verdicts or settlements above a million dollars.

"Like tennis and golf, there are only a few who have both the talent and the disposition to do it well," says Federal District Court Judge William Hoeveler, who as a defense trial lawyer some years ago battled Mr. Spence many times. "When you find both, as you do in J.B., those are the ones who win."

Dissecting expertise, of course, can be a tricky undertaking. Mr. Spence, however, clearly creates some of his own advantages. He benefits from his selectivity: He turns down 20 cases for every one he accepts. In addition, many in the local legal community cite his uncanny knack for selecting jurors. Although juries are supposed to be a cross section of the population, they tend to be dominated by ordinary workaday people simply because there are so many of them. Even then, Mr. Spence proceeds carefully.

"When you pick a good jury, the case is 90% won," he contends, adding: "I can just about look at a person and tell if I want him as a juror. If he has Gucci loafers, a Rolex watch and a Kiwanis pin, he has his, and he has no heart for the underdog. He doesn't believe in the jury system, he doesn't like lawyers, and he's afraid of being sued. He may be the backbone of America, but he's not going to sit on my jury."

Instead, Mr. Spence says, "I'm looking for heart, the guy in a corduroy jacket, with no tie and reading a paperback." He loves to have warmhearted grandmothers on his juries. But he's skeptical of female jurors when the plaintiff is an attractive woman. "As a general rule, they're jealous," he asserts.

Key to Success

At 5 feet 7 inches and 160 pounds, Mr. Spence doesn't present an imposing figure to his workaday jurors. "I don't look like a lawyer, and I don't talk like a lawyer—I'm not polished," he says. He says he has overheard other attorneys disparage him. Asked what single trait accounts most for his success, he responds, "I understand people."

In some ways, that isn't surprising.

Orphaned at 16, he grew up in northwest Florida with his grandfather, a tenant farmer who worked other people's land for a share of the crops. The boy, whose birth certificate says "unnamed Spence child," got his only surnames—so the story goes—after someone suggested, "Let's call him J.B." He says he grew up in a house "so far back in the woods we used to gather on the porch to watch a car go by." He plowed afoot behind a mule, picked cotton and hoed peanuts.

At 17, he ran away—and ended up in the Navy. For six years, starting before Pearl Harbor, the Navy would be family, and, for four years, the destroyer USS Gary would be home.

In 1946, he left the Navy, a 24-year-old high-school dropout lacking direction and any marketable skill. For 18 months, he mowed lawns, sold cars, painted houses and drove a laundry truck—but his status began to gnaw at him. "I was sick of gathering people's dirty laundry, and I hated taking orders," he says. It was then that a Veterans Administration advisor observed, "J.B., you're going to be a flunky all your life unless you get an education."

A Quick Study

Life changed swiftly. Roughly three years from starting night classes to finish high school, he graduated cum laude from the University of Miami Law School. He almost quit law school once, bored by the tedium of a real-estate course. But the theatrical atmosphere of a crowded courtroom excited him. After a stint as an assistant attorney general, he attracted the attention of Perry Nichols, a famed personal-injury lawyer with whom he worked for 15 years before striking out on his own.

From his background, the Nichols tutelage and the grind of handling "dreg" cases, he developed his courtroom style. "Some attorneys are arrogant, some are nasty, and a few are vicious," observes George Lanza, a defense attorney who has often faced Mr. Spence. "J.B. is humble.

He's the guy next door, sincere and honest. He comes across like he's discussing the case with a bunch of people in his living room."

But courtroom drama, presented with persuasive, emotion-stirring oratory, is a Spence trademark. "He's not movie-actor dramatic—he's not Melvin Belli—but he knows how to convey his case to the jury," says Administrative Judge John Gale. Mr. Lanza recalls Mr. Spence representing a young model who lost a leg in a medical-malpractice case: "He stripped her down to her shorts, and, with that leg hanging there, he argued her case. The jury went for $3.4 million."

Mr. Spence's clients often take off clothing just before defendants lose their shirts. In 1985, he represented a young beautician who set herself on fire and was badly burned over her upper body. She sued her psychiatrist, arguing that she had already tried suicide once and he should have hospitalized her to protect her.

Showing Off Scars

Over the defense attorney's violent objections, Mr. Spence had her strip down to her bra and panties and display scars that even he calls "gruesome." The jury, impressed, ordered $2.1 million. (However, the judge set the verdict aside, saying "psychiatrists and psychologists…have no measurable superior ability to predict human conduct." The case is on appeal.)

Observes another veteran of battles with Mr. Spence, attorney George Mitchell, "I never tried a case with J.B. when he didn't put the widow on the stand."

His style soon began impressing jurors. "When J.B. came on the scene, there were almost no malpractice decisions against doctors," recalls Howard Barwick, a defense attorney. "He won a malpractice award of $100,000 in the 1960s when six-figure verdicts were unheard of for anything—and that sent up a flag. Medical malpractice cases increased greatly after that." In 1967, Mr. Spence won a jury award of $1.5 million, which he says was the first Florida personal-injury award to top a million dollars.

Although medical-malpractice cases account for some 90% of his work, he uses emotional tactics in other litigation as well. In a case involving the death of an eight-year-old girl killed by a truck, Mr. Spence put on the witness stand her younger sister, a lovely blond child of seven, who read a poem she had composed about how much she missed her sister. "I deal with a very raw slice of life," he notes.

As his court victories piled up, defense attorneys became leery of him. In final arguments, one told the jury: "I am concerned about the obvious excellent speaking ability of Mr. Spence. He is an excellent orator. He can be very passionate. He may cry and try to get any of you to cry during his closing remarks. That is very difficult to combat." Mr. Spence did cry—and so did much of the jury, which then voted a multimillion-dollar award.

While empathy for victims drives him, so does antipathy for doctors. "One reason I enjoy suing them is the colossal ego and arrogance I see, the holier-than-thou attitude that because they save lives that gives them the privilege to get away with it [malpractice] once," he fumes.

Mr. Spence says he and his family have never had a firsthand problem with bad doctors, but he concedes that he is anti-establishment, "very strongly so." He comments, "I can't stand pomposity at any quarter, whether lawyers, judges, or whatever. But for absolute pomposity, doctors are No. 1—America's only nobility. Who else walks into a restaurant and presents his title, 'I'm Doctor Jones'?"

His antipathy for doctors is reciprocated. One unsuccessfully sued him for libel in 1984 after he criticized the physician in a speech to a hospital staff. He says he was booed off stage by the University of Miami Medical School after being invited to talk there. And he says that when a son—one of his four children—was injured in a football game, the boy was turned away by a hospital when its officials learned who he was. Mr. Spence also has abruptly left some cocktail parties after being insulted by some medical people.

But to remind himself of his fallibility, he regularly reviews a file labeled "J.B.'s Blunders," errors he made in court. One, he recalls, was a case he lost after selecting an Army colonel as a juror. "That was a one-man jury," Mr. Spence complains. "He dominated other jurors, and he convinced everybody that what I presented was physically impossible."

That was more than two decades ago, but to this day Mr. Spence, when walking into court to pick a jury in a major case, carries in his pocket a slip of paper that says "no colonels."

An 'Unpopular' Law Practice is Profitable

They's flies on you
And they's flies on me,
But there ain't no flies
On The Great J.B."
…popular legend

By FRED McCORMACK
Herald—Tribune Staff Writer

J.B. Spence is a soft-spoken country boy who makes about $1 million a year doing what he thinks is just as unpopular as suing Santa Claus.

He's a specialist in what he calls the most difficult legal field in the world. Every time he enters a new town to practice his specialty he feels like Daniel in the lion's den.

Spence is an expert in medical malpractice law. He sues doctors and hospitals for negligence and more often that not, wins cash settlements for his clients.

It's not the most popular of professional pursuits.

"You can safely say that I may not be the most popular man in town when I'm trying a case," he says. "In some of these cases, I feel that if I got hurt in an accident and somebody took me to a hospital emergency room I'd get the deep six instead of medical treatment."

Spence was in Sarasota last week conducting the five-day long courtroom trial which culminated his two-year-old negligence suit against a local physician and the Sarasota Memorial Hospital.

Nobody expected a major judgement, even though Spence was seeking $1 million in damages. Florida's west coast, almost any negligence lawyer in the state will vow, is notorious for meager judgments.

But in this case, the six-person jury deliberated for less than two hours and gave Spence's client $350,000, the largest such award in county history. The client promptly fainted and Spence came close to it himself.

Suing a doctor, says Spence, is just like suing Santa Claus. It's the most difficult thing in the world and it represents the biggest legal challenge he knows of.

Spence is one of 21 men in the nation who are good enough at negligence work to have brought in judgements of $1 million or more.

He also brought in the highest single judgement in United States history—$3 million against the Dominican Republic airlines after an airplane owned by that company crashed into a Miami paint shop and killed two young boys.

There is only one other negligence attorney in Spence's league—a Californian named Bruce Walkup—and while Walkup has won more cases, Spence brings in bigger judgments.

Spence and men like him have had a profound impact on the medical profession. They've made physicians, nurses, hospital administrators, and just about everybody connected with the healing arts acutely aware of the threat of a lawsuit if something goes awry in patient treatment.

There's an old story that purports to describe a Florida doctor's greatest fear: J.B. Spence pulling up in his Cadillac.

Spence, in person, is the antithesis of the high-powered trail lawyer. He's no F. Lee Bailey, Melvin Belli or Percy Foreman. He's a simple-living man, he says, a fella who'd rather go fishing than night-clubbing. He never seeks publicity and as a trial is about to begin, when many attorneys conduct a whirlwind courtship of the press, Spence goes out of his way to stay out of sight.

Most people who see him are struck at once by his resemblance to President Richard M. Nixon. Dye his blonde, curly hair black, give him a few inches in height and a heavier beard and the resemblance would be uncanny.

Although he can shout and gesticulate with the best of them when he objects to a point of law or procedure in the courtroom, his usual style is low-key.

"I think people expect to see me pull a rabbit out of a hat in the courtroom," says Spence. "They don't expect me to just go about my job quietly and methodically, maybe like a farmer or perhaps a house painter. But that's just what I do."

PROCLAMATION

J.B. Spence

Whereas, J. B. Spence has been a highly respected member in good standing of The Florida Bar since February 5, 1951; and

Whereas, J. B. Spence is of counsel to Leeds & Colby, P.A., and was a partner in Spence, Payne, Masington, Needle & Leeds from 1968-1995, where he has ably served clients who are victims of personal injury, wrongful death, medical malpractice, defective products, and aviation, automobile, railroad and admiralty cases; and

Whereas, J. B. Spence has long been a devoted public servant, working as Assistant Attorney General for the State of Florida and as Assistant State Attorney for Dade County and serving on the Nominating Commission of the Third District Court of Appeal and Florida's Constitution Revision Commission; and

Whereas, J. B. Spence received his law degree from the University of Miami where he later served as an adjunct professor at the School of Law, and one year following his graduation and admission to The Florida Bar was also admitted to practice law before the U.S. District Court, Southern District of Florida, and to the U.S. Supreme Court; and

Whereas, J. B. Spence is a respected faculty member of the National College of Advocacy, is a guest lecturer at Harvard Law School, is a frequent speaker at bar association meetings on the art and science of the final argument, and is the author of numerous articles published in respected legal journals; and

Whereas, J. B. Spence is an active member of the American Bar Association, the Association of Trial Lawyers of America, the International Academy of Trial Lawyers, the Law Science Academy and the prestigious Inner Circle of Advocates; and

Whereas, J. B. Spence is listed in *The Best Lawyers in America* and has been recognized for his highly distinguished professional career with the J. B. Spence Scholarship at the University of Miami School of Law; and

Whereas, J. B. Spence is known for his unwavering compassion for his clients and for his complete dedication to each case and every client he represents; and

Whereas, J. B. Spence is known by Florida lawyers as a mentor, a colleague and a friend, as well as a respected leader in the field of law.

Now therefore, be it resolved, that the Board of Governors of The Florida Bar, on behalf of the nearly 70,000 lawyers in this state, commend, laud and honor J. B. Spence for his 50 years of distinguished service and his many lasting contributions to the law, for his meritorious service to the legal profession, and for his dedication to the people of this great state.

Dated this 12th day of April, 2001.

Herman J. Russomanno
President, 2000-2001

CHAPTER 5

My Disaster

There's a story around town among divorce lawyers as follows: A divorce lawyer represents a young woman married to an older man who is successful, wealthy and well-established.

She decides that she would like a divorce and to get everything she can. So, the hypothetical lawyer tells the story of another young woman under similar circumstances who decided to get a divorce and that hypothetical lawyer pointed out to his client that, if she had a domestic dispute, she could start a fight and provoke him to protect himself and get the husband to strike her.

If that didn't make a big enough imprint, to scratch herself or tear her clothes and become disheveled, and call the police.

The husband is arrested, taken to jail and charged with a felony to rob him of his license to practice law or, if he were a doctor, to practice medicine, and now has a criminal charge against him.

Then on the Monday after these events occur on Saturday, he is served with the divorce papers and a few days later he is served with papers for a tort action.

Three lawsuits at one time, stories all over the paper, and the hypothetical wife retains a team of lawyers for each case.

I had remarried, this was the third time, in San Francisco on a sailboat under the Golden Gate Bridge, on Valentine's Day, a true Irish romance.

Sadly, however, this marriage had no soul. It was full of deceit, greed and betrayal, the absolute worse mistake of my life.

I went through a similar scenario. Me, a naïve, childlike, trusting person. The majority of the lawyers descended upon me as if I were a carcass and they were vultures.

The attorneys' fees were incredible. A huge fee game was played notwithstanding the judge repeatedly saying, "Let's shorten this, cut all of the costs down and let's just put this behind us."

I lost my home on Key Biscayne, I lost my boats, my law firm collapsed, and just before all of this happened, I had purchased an enormously beautiful residence, a gated mansion on the prestigious Davis Road, and my wife had on the same day bought herself a new black Jaguar convertible.

Everything had been well-planned, a clever setup. Mountains of legal work, tort, divorce, crime, law firm. Unbelievable.

I received letters addressed to "O. J. Spence" and I could see people whispering everywhere I went, and the newspapers were full of long stories about me, the successful trial lawyer with the abused wife.

My health took a terrible turn, serious depression, great loss of weight, emotionally disturbed.

Many people came to my rescue and stood by me. I am grateful for all of that help.

There were three female Assistant State Attorneys assigned to my case. They were lusting to convict. They wanted my scalp, their victory on their resumes.

Their behavior was almost hysterical. They bounced around the courtroom like three teenage cheerleaders. "Conviction, conviction, conviction" was their song and when they took my housekeeper's deposition, they asked her, "How frequently do you have sex with Mr. Spence?" Petty behavior, sad, cheap.

One of the moments I'll never, ever forget is the scene in the Criminal Court when the State Attorney's Office had offered me a deal: If I would plead guilty to the charges, attend an anger management school, pay a 25,000 dollar fine and pick up trash on the roadside, they would dismiss the case.

As all of this was being said, I glanced at the back of the courtroom and there sat my still-wife, and she mouthed the words to me "FU."

All of this was being televised, and the judge spoke saying, "Mr. Spence, what is your choice, plead guilty or go to trial?"

My dear friend and wonderful attorney said, "J. B., this is your decision."

I walked to the podium and paused for a second. I felt like I was standing on the edge of a razor blade, my whole life on the table.

If I did not accept the State Attorney's proposal, tried the case and lost it, I would be a convicted felon and disbarred.

I told the judge I would put my faith in the hands of a jury. Shortly thereafter, the State Attorney nol-prossed the suit, dismissed it and the nightmare went away.

We live and learn. I'm looking forward to and I want to be in the courtroom trying lawsuits, protecting innocent victims, taking on the greedy, mean, dishonest, cruel corporate America.

When Congress and state legislatures are owned by corporate America, profits come first, people's Constitutional rights are brushed aside.

The only hope for justice is the trial lawyers. We fight corporate America in the courtroom and win because of the law. The Constitution, without the trial lawyers, would be a disaster.

However, we have a problem, which is our image as trial lawyers. We're no longer seen as a service profession which assists injured and disabled people.

The term "Personal Injury Trial Lawyer" has become a derogatory one. The public generally describes us as greedy. We have a difficult time trying to show our better side. Few people know the positive side.

We have done an enormous amount of work for the people of our state. Last year alone, Florida trial lawyers devoted nearly one million hours of pro bono work, almost two million dollars of legal aid.

We hope to educate the public and prove we are entitled to be known as serious fighters for the Rule of Law, or corporate greed would control America as I think it does now.

My life has been absolutely fantastic, a pleasure, a joy, simply wonderful.

Recently, I took a yellow pad, I drew a line down the middle and on one side, I put the word "gratitude," on the other side I put the word "accomplishments."

I discussed accomplishments from being president of four legal associations, serving on the Constitution Revision Commission, serving on the Judicial Qualifications Commission, the incredible

Street Journal story, teaching at Harvard, the Perry Nichols award, writing a book on final argument, teaching at the University of Miami, lecturing across the nation, having a very successful law practice, being surrounded by wonderful, caring, generous partners, having the respect of the community. And all of that has been simply wonderful.

On the other side, the gratitude list is enormous: Two wonderful, loving wives who each gave me great comfort, great support, great happiness and moments that I will treasure all of my life; two children by my first wife, Patricia; two children by my second wife, Mary Jo.

These children, Mark, Martha, John and Gary, are very special to me. They have filled my life with joy and pleasure and love and still do.

I am grateful for many other things, for knowing God, for having good health and having the passion that I do to practice law and to help innocent victims against the greed and horror of corporate America.

I am asked repeatedly why I continue to practice law. I have no answer for that question, but I do know why. It is the memory of all of the tragic cases, the innocent victims.

I am very grateful for my life as a trial lawyer. I have been fortunate to help others.

In closing, I say thanks. Thanks to all of you who have shared my life with me. Thanks.

Happy The Man

Happy the man, and happy he alone,
He who can call today his own:
He who, secure within, can say,
Tomorrow do thy worst, for I have lived today.
Be fair or foul or rain or shine
The joys I have possessed, in spite of fate,
Are mine.
Not Heaven itself upon the past has power,
But what has been, has been, and I have had my hour.

— John Dryden
(9 August 1631—1 May 1700)

J. B. SPENCE

Born March the 31st, 1922
Russellville, Arkansas.

***

Legal education, University of Miami,
February 1951, graduated Magna cum laude.

***

Served in the U.S. Navy in both the
Atlantic and Pacific Theaters during World War II

**

Awarded six Navy wartime medals.

***

Served as Assistant Attorney General of the State of Florida

***

President of the Dade County Bar.

***

President of the Academy of
Florida Trial Lawyers.
President of the American Board of
Professional Liability Lawyers.
President Emeritus—Honor, Dade County
Trial Lawyers Association.

***

Fellow of the American College of Trial Lawyers.

***

Fellow of the International Academy of Trial Lawyers.

***

Advocate, American Board of
Trial Advocates.
Fellow, International Society of
Trial Barristers.

***

Member of the Association of
Trial Lawyers of America.

***

Inner Circle of Advocates, founding member.

***

Adjunct Professor,
University of Miami Law School.

***

Recipient of the
Perry Nichols Award.

***

Recipient of the Al J. Cone
Distinguished Leadership Award.

***

Member of the Law Science Academy.

***

Chairman of the Medical Malpractice
Committee of the Association of
Trial Lawyers of America.

***

Assistant State Attorney, Miami, Florida.

***

Member of the Judicial Nominating Commission of the Third
District Court of Appeal.

***

Member of the Constitution Revision Commission,
State of Florida.

***

Voted Top Trial Lawyer in Miami by
Bar Association and Judiciary.

***

Faculty member,
National College of Advocacy.

***

Won more than 100 cases with a verdict of a million dollars
or more in Personal injury and malpractice cases.

***

Won the first million-dollar verdict in Florida.

***

Author of the book, *Final Argument.*

***

Awarded the Certificate of Distinction by
The Florida Bar.

***

Served as a Florida Ombudsman.

***

Guest lecturer at many law schools throughout the country.
***

Spoke many times on national television
regarding medical malpractice.

***

Proctor in Admiralty Sinking of the YARMOUTH CASTLE.
***

PERRY NICHOLS

822 ALFONSO AVENUE

CORAL GABLES, FLORIDA 33146

August 8, 1978

Dear JB:

    Congratulations on being selected the
outstanding personal injury lawyer in Miami.
You deserve every word they wrote about you and
I am as proud of you as if you were my son.

    It certainly is nice to be remembered by
old associates and friends.

    Best personal regards,

            Sincerely,

            Perry Nichols

J. B. Spence, Esq.
801 City National Bank Building
Miami, Florida 33130

§ 2-6 Plaintiff's closing argument and rebuttal RE: Medical malpractice case involving the death of a wife and mother

COMMENT: The following is an argument made by Mr. J.B. Spence

Are you ready to proceed, Mr. Spence?

MR. SPENCE: Yes, Your Honor. May it please the Court, counsel for the defense, ladies, sir, we are at the end of the case and we are permitted at this time to visit with you for a few minutes about what we think the significant and important evidence is in the case.

Technically, this part of the case is called final argument. I do not plan to make an argument. I think we are way past arguing and it is a time for the decision. It is the time for you all to decide and it is time for you to decide this case according to the oath that you took as jurors a long, long time ago, that you would try the case well and true, according to the law and the evidence.

At this point in time I would like to get all of the personalities out of the way, all of the anger, all of the hostilities, all of the shouting, and try to help you, if I may, look at the key evidence in this case. If I had all day, I could talk about the lawsuit, but I am going to boil it down to what I think is the heart of the case, the key evidence in the case, the important evidence in the case and ask you to please follow me, if you would, while I review this with you. This is an important part of the case.

Now, you have all merely seen a tip of an iceberg, even though you have been here for a very long three weeks. We flew may places and spent many hours, and way into the night, taking those 40 depositions, so that we knew what everyone was going to say. Many days, many hours, many nights, working, working, working, so that we could bring you the truth in this case and that you would know where the justice is in this case.

That is all behind us now and we are at a point now where we are going to talk about the evidence. The Judge is going to tell you what the law is, and you are all going to decide the case according to the oath that you took, on the law and the evidence, not personalities. Not who is the most handsome or the ugliest or the best lawyer or the worst lawyer, but where is the truth in this case between Orlando Silva and his family, and all of these defendants, with respect to Teresita Silva being wrongfully killed in this case. That is where we are at this point.

I am going to do my best to stay in the bull's eye, not wander over the wide world about everything, but come back to the bull's eye.

I need to make a couple of preliminary remarks. One, we thank you, and this is not said to butter you up, but we thank you from the bottom of our hearts for the sacrifice you have made. I know it has been a big one, to sit here all of this time.

My clients, Orlando Silva and his family, who are seated here, thank you for the interest that you have made and the sacrifice that you have made to make the American jury system work, so we thank you and we appreciate it.

Now, bear in mind, please, this is a civil suit, not a criminal case. No one is going to jail. This is a civil suit, approved by the Supreme Court of this state, and the legislature of this state to compensate someone, for paying money to someone for the grief and anguish and the heartache and the destruction that has occurred. It is a civil suit for money damage for each one of those five claimants.

This has been like a teeter-totter in this case. That is what it has been. Up and down, up and down.

We do not have to have a photograph of where that tube was. Just a reasonable doubt. We have to prove our case by which side is more probably telling you the truth.

Where is the truth in this case? It is like putting it on a scale. One weighs 51 and one weighs 49. The heavier side. That is the rule of this case. It is all we are required to do. We believe we have done a great deal more than that.

It is the heavier side with the quality of the evidence, not the number of the evidence, the number of the witnesses that side tilts over.

It is like in football. If the score is five to four, the five wins because it is more believable, more credible and more likely. Now, that is all we have to do here. Please do not ask us to do more than that. In a civil suit, that is all we have to do. If we tilt the scales more than a majority, we are entitled to win under the law in this state.

Now, these remarks I am making, I am not saying them, but they are important in my judgment to the case. I have lived with this lawsuit. I feel like I am ten years older. I never ever, as long as I live, want to try another lawsuit like this. It is something like –

MR. SEVIER: Excuse me. I am sorry, Mr. Spence. I would have to make the same comment and give the same emotion about my feeling for my clients.

THE COURT: Mr. Spence, let us get on with it.

MR. SPENCE: Forgive me. I will do my best not to let that happen to me again, but let us go to Chapter One. Let us go to that operating room on August the 24th, 1978, and let us find out what those people have to say that were there, those eyewitnesses that were there. Those people that were there, not the hard experts that fly down here from someplace to give you an opinion on the matter, our experts, their experts. Let us go to the eyewitnesses that saw this terrible disaster occur in that operating room.

Who are they? Dr. Cruz was there, and she has told you that this poor lady was dead on the table. She had no pulse. The monitor was flat. Her abdomen was distended. She had cyanosis. She was not breathing. She had no heartbeat. That is why she went to get Orlando Silva. She knew his wife was dead on the table. Dr. Cruz, the first witness, said those things.

On the other side of Dr. Cruz is Dr. Gurvich over there who says, "Help me. I am in big trouble and I have a flexible memory, Raquel."

As between Dr. Cruz and Dr. Gurvich, where is the credibility and who do you choose to believe between those two people? Cruz or Gurvich.

The next person in that room, Dr. Mainieri, he said, "This patient was dead. The monitor was flat. There were no pulses. She was cyanotic. She had no heartbeat. She was not breathing and I tried to give her some cardiac massage."

Dr Mainieri. He was there. He saw it. The first person to get to her, the first person to try to get her back alive, trying to put in some air. Who are you going to believe? Mainieri or Dr. Gurvich? Who says, "Help me. I am in big trouble and I have a flexible memory, Raquel. I will come and testify you did not do anything wrong. How about helping me? I am in big trouble and I have a flexible memory."

Who are you going to believe between Dr. Mainieri on one hand

and Dr. Gurvich on the other hand, and the next witness who was there at the first inning, in that operating room when this whole thing started, Dr, Rodriguez and what does Dr. Rodriguez tell you? He is one of the doctors that flew off to Spain. We had to read you his deposition, but he said, "This lady was dead on the table. She had no pulse, no heartbeat, a flat line of the monitor. Cardiac arrest."

As between Dr. Rodriguez on one hand and Dr. Gurvich over here, who says, Help me. I am in big trouble, big trouble down at the Courthouse. I have got a flexible memory. Bail me out. I was incompetent. I was negligent. I was careless. I did not do what I was supposed to do and I let her die on the table, but help me, Raquel. I have got a flexible memory."

Who are you going to believe? Rodriguez or Gurvich on what was going on in that operating room?

Dr. Escar. Dr. Escar is an employee of this hospital. The assistant surgeon. He was the fellow we had on the stand there that we had to have an interpreter in here to say what he said.

What did he say? The blood was dark. Then it turned black. Then she went into cardiac arrest. She had no pulse. She was dead on the table. There was a flat line on the monitor. She was not breathing, no heartbeat.

I said, " What brought on all of this?" He said, "Because the tube was in the wrong place. The tube was in the wrong place." That is what he said. "Her abdomen was distended and she was dead because she did not have any oxygen."

Who are you going to believe between Escar and Gurvich on that? Escar, who was there and saw it with his own eyes, as well as Dr. Cruz and as well as Dr, Mainieri, as well as Dr. Rodriguez, or are you going to believe Dr. Gurvich over here, who says, "Help me. I am in trouble. I have got a flexible memory."? You know, which one's credibility? The Judge says that you look him in the eye. You make up your mind who is telling the truth, who has an axe to grind in this case, who is trying to protect himself and who, in fact, is in trouble, so here you have a choice, ladies and sir. Escar, Rodriguez, Mainieri, Cruz said all of those things. Gurvich, you know what he says.

Then, lo and behold, there is a disaster. Orlando Silva, seated in the doctors' lounge, having a cup of coffee, visiting. Can you imagine how this man felt? Sitting there, an innocent person who did not ask for all of this grief to be brought around his ears? She said, "Orlando, Orlando. Come. She is not breathing. She is dead."

He runs in this room. He did some things. Well, he kicked his shoes off. Are we going to send him to jail because he kicked his shoes off? He kicked his shoes off outside. He comes in the room. He said, "Oh, God, no. No. Is she dead? Is she gone?"

Then, they want to say he killed his own wife on top of all that. That is mind-boggling to me. That is incredible to me that they would point the finger to Orlando Silva, say, "Go back to the doctors' lounge. Do not come and see your wife dying. We will take care of her."

They were not taking very good care of her. None of them were taking care of her. This is the worst thing I've ever seen with respect to hospital care, medical care and doctor care. That fellow is incompetent over there.

MR. KUTNER: Objection.

THE COURT: Sustained.

MR. KUTNER: Appropriate motion, Your Honor.

MR. SPENCE: Forgive me.

You have got Dr. Cruz, Dr. Escar, Dr. Mainieri, Dr. Rodriguez. You have poor Dr. Silva there who walks in there and finds his wife cyanotic, a distended abdomen as big as is she was pregnant, because it is full of air, and he drums his finger on her stomach as it is distended full of air. I don't remember what the fancy word they gave that was, but it was like tapping a balloon full of air.

He says, "What is going on here? What are you people doing?", and he said she was dead and nothing on the monitor and no breath sounds and he turns to Dr. Gurvich and says, "You have got the tube in the wrong place. You have got the tube in the wrong place. You are putting the oxygen that ought to be going into her lungs to make her breathe, you are putting in her stomach. Please do something about this. Take the tube out. Change the tube. Will you, please?"

Finally, he does, and after he takes that tube out and puts it back in, there is a great change in what is going on in this patient. Shortly, she can be ventilated. Shortly, her heart is beating. Shortly, her cyanosis goes away and she returns, and the fact that she is breathing, but her brain has been destroyed. It has been destroyed. You have those five people on the one hand there. Cruz, Escar, Mainieri, Rodriguez and Silva tell you what was going on in that operating room and who do we have over here that says, "Oh, no. This is all crazy. This is all imagination." We have Dr. Gurvich, the same Dr. Gurvich who says, "Help me. I am in trouble. I have got a flexible memory, Raquel. I will come and testify that you didn't do anything wrong, but help me. Help me. I am the man with the airway. I am the man that let her die. I am the man that did not give her the oxygen, but help me."

Then, we go to the things that lawyers have to do. We have to get ourselves an expert or two experts, because you jurors are presumed to be ignorant about all of this, and the law compels us to get experts to come and tell you, did they do it right or did they do it wrong, and we have this little fancy phrase that I discussed in the beginning. Did they depart from the accepted practices of medical care? That is the same thing as saying were they careless? Were they negligent and did they do it wrong, so we brought Professor Zauder down here. Dr. Zauder, a big man in anesthesia, worldwide known. He says, "The tube was in the wrong place. The tube was in the esophagus. There was no bronchospasm. That is an invention. That is an alibi. That is an old wives' tale."

That is the Easter Bunny. A bronchospasm is, in this case, and he says, "Gurvich is negligent and the hospital is negligent and they all departed from acceptable medical care and they are all careless and they are all responsible."

Then, we brought you Dr. Forthman. You remember Dr. Forthman. That is the fellow, he and I owned a boat together many years ago. I guess because we owned a boat together many years ago, I am going to be able to persuade Dr. Forthman to come down here and give you a cock-and-bull story, a fairy tale.

He sat up on the stand, 30 years of experience. He used to give it at Cedars. Remember, the big heavyset fellow, kind of nervous? A nice guy.

He says to you folks, "No bronchospasm in this case. No bronchospasm in this case. Gurvich is negligent. Gurvich is careless.

Gurvich departed from accepted medical care," and then he showed you how, when you have an endotracheal tube in the esophagus, it does not have a seal; that you can breathe all day long. You would not explode somebody's stomach. You would not blow them off the table. You would not float them in the room.

He said, "The only way you would know is listening carefully, because the air goes around and comes out silently."

Are you going to believe Dr. Forthman, Dr. Zauder, about 60 years of anesthesia experience about where the truth is in this case, or are you going to believe Dr. Gurvich over there, who is in trouble, who wants some help from Raquel over here and has a flexible memory? You know, just tell me what to say and I will sing a song here and get myself out of this, if I have the capability of fooling the jury.

Cullen, their own witness. Their own witness, that they flew down here. The anesthesiologist said, "I would have pulled the tube out a great deal sooner."

Flor, the last fellow. We read his deposition yesterday, the last deposition. Flor, who practices at American Hospital, the Chief of Anesthesia there, who did not want to be in this case and who did not want to be involved and who did not want to read these records, and says, "I know all of these defendants. I know Shelly Munach. I know Steiner. Do not get me into this. Do not make me tell you what I really think," and Shelly Munach calls him up and says, "Remi, this is a bronchospasm case. You really do not want to be in this case. You really do not want to do that to your friends," and Remi says, "I am sorry. I must tell the truth. If it destroys our friendship, I am sorry, and Shelly, if you want to play it that way, a bronchospasm, doctor to doctor, go do it, but I know better and you know better. There was no bronchospasm in this case."

Now, you think about that. You also think about this. If this man was not a doctor and he was not there, he was just an ordinary plain citizen. He had a phone call that night. "Doctor, I would hate to tell you. Your wife did not take the anesthesia too well. I am really sorry about it." Mr. Silva, not Dr. Silva, but "Your wife did not take the anesthesia too well." That would have been the end of it, you see, but fate somehow put him in there in that doctors' lounge. Fate enabled him to have two of his friends there, Dr. Mainieri and Dr. Rodriguez. Fate allowed Dr. Escar to tell the truth about what went on, and fate put Raquel Cruz there, who delivered two of his four children, seated back there, the two little ones there, Carlos and Jorge.

Raquel said, "I do not want to say the tube was in the wrong place. Do not push me into that. I do not want to do that," but she says, "I have to tell you the tube was in the wrong place." That is Dr. Cruz, and on and on and on.

Dr. Lopez says the tube was in the wrong place. No oxygen, brain destroyed ten to 15, 20 minutes with no oxygen. This poor man goes out and tells Dr. Lopez, he says, "Put something to my brain and take it in there and put it on my wife's brain. See if you can't jump my brain to her brain and start her back to life again." This is when he made those crazy threats that he was going to kill somebody, and I apologize for him and I do not penalize him for it. That is wrong to say you are going to kill somebody, but people do feel strongly about losing a loved one, that was done carelessly and wrongfully and negligently, and then they try to cover it up. Not only kill her, but then try to cover it up.

The brain is destroyed in three or four or five minutes. Finally, the heart says, "I cannot handle living without oxygen and I quit, too," and his wife did not have any oxygen for ten or fifteen minutes. Her brain was destroyed, dead, killed. Then, finally the heart said, "I cannot go any further without oxygen and I quit, too," and that is when he was brought to the room, after his wife's heart had quit, because she did not have any oxygen.

Dr. Wright, the Dade County Medical Examiner, said she was without oxygen for ten or 20 minutes. Total destruction of her brain. This man has done about 4,000 autopsies in this county. He said he has never heard of a bronchospasm killing somebody.

A young, healthy, strong, beautiful woman goes in the hospital for a simple surgery. This is not a heart implant or this is not nine hours on the table. This is something that is going to be done to women and have been done every day, and then they go on back home to their husband and their children and they are not killed in an operating room.

He never hear of a bronchospasm. He said this machine has a pop-off valve. He never heard of a stomach ruptured like that.

Then we flew down a doctor from Harvard. We got Dr. Emmanuel Friedman, one of the greatest OB-GYN people in the world. He said these nurses—we have dropped the nurses from the case. The Court will rule that the hospital is responsible for whatever they did or for whatever they did not do. I do not want their names on the verdict with you thinking that there is some way they are going to have to pay anything in this case. They are out of the lawsuit, because the Court has ruled that whatever they did or did not do, the hospital is responsible for it, because they were employees of the hospital. Nurse Randolph's name is not on that verdict and Nurse Gianniny's name is not on the verdict.

Dr. Emmanuel Friedman said everybody in that operating room, those nurses, Dr. Escar, all of them were responsible. They should have called a Code Blue a great deal earlier.

Now, I want to move to something that you may say to yourself, "Why has Mr. Spence spent so much time on this? Why, back in voir dire, three weeks ago, was he asking us, have you heard the phrase ostensible agent, apparent agent, agent, and you had to say to yourself, in my opening statement, when I suddenly shifted off of all of the medicine and got over talking about agency, an ostensible agent and an apparent agent, "What is the significance of that?", and that is one of the most vital points in this case, and on this verdict form that the Judge is going to hand you, the first question that you will answer that is: "Do you find that Dr. Ruben Gurvich was an agent," "An agent of Cedars of Lebanon Hospital?", "Yes" or "No."

"Do you find that he was an agent at the time that he was in that room giving that anesthesia?" Do you find he was an agent? First question, "Yes" or "no."

I ask you to vote, "Yes," that he was an agent of the hospital. That is a very, very, very vital issue in this case, the agency, because the hospital is responsible for whatever an agent does that is careless.

I repeat that the hospital is responsible for what all of their employees do that is careless or wrong. The Judge will tell you that the hospital is responsible for what an agent does and what an agent does not do, if it is careless or negligent, that the hospital is responsible for their employees. The hospital is responsible for their agents. That is the first question the Judge will give you. He will give you a definition of agency, of what an agent is. This is the first question on this verdict form and I ask you to say, "Yes, he was an agent. He was agent of the hospital." These are the reasons that I ask you to vote "Yes" on that, and write, "Yes, he was an agent."

It is true he was not on the payroll, but they had an arrangement there, a quid pro quo arrangement, the hospital and the anesthesiologist did, where these anesthesiologists were everyday covering ten operating rooms, doing 5,000 operations a year. Every operation needs an anesthesiologist, and this is really an enormous amount of money that that hospital is taking in because of those 5,000 operations and 5,000 anesthesias, and they cannot function with those 700 beds out there unless they have got people helping them, people representing them and an agent is a person who helps someone and who represents them.

When Dr. Capati—let me have one of those coats please – walked in there, with whichever one of these coats that says – the other one, please—she walks in there with this coat on that says, "Cedars of Lebanon Hospital, Surgery," and the other one says, "Anesthesia," on it, and a patient is in bed and a total stranger walks in. "I am your anesthesiologist. I am with Cedars Anesthesiology Department. I am with Cedars Anesthesiology Department." That person at that time is an agent of that hospital. They are acting for the hospital. They are representing the hospital. They are furthering the hospital's business. They are flying the flag of the hospital and they are asserting that they are an agent of the hospital, that "I represent the hospital and I am here." They have about 1,300 employees out there in this hospital, and you do not stop one of them who comes in and says, "I am going to take the chest X-ray" and they have got "Cedars" on their coat, you do not say, "Get your ID card out. I mean, who you are, where you came from and what is your arrangement for the hospital? Do you have a contract in your pocket? Do you have some kind of a secret deal? Tell me about it."

Patients do not do that. You go in there and you trust them to do what is right for you. They take a chest X-ray, get your ID card, who do you work for? The nurse comes in to give you your medicine or the people who come to tell you, you have got to have a soapsuds enema or the lab people or the Pathology Department, all of the departments out there, they advertise they are Cedars' services. Cedars' employees. Cedars' agents. This is a very, very vital issue in this case, the question of agency.

All kinds of secret deals they have made have no effect on Mrs. Silva or Dr. Silva, who did not know anything about these arrangements. They had the perfect right to assume when Dr. Capati said, "I am from Cedars' Anesthesiology Department," that she is telling the truth and Mrs. Silva had the perfect right to assume when that fellow came out in the greens and said, "I am your anesthesiologist. We are going in." They were part and parcel of Cedars' team. Whether anybody was on the payroll or not does not make any difference. It is, were they representing Cedars? Were they a part of Cedars' business? Were they a representative of Cedars, and when you are wearing that coat and you tell somebody, "I am from Cedars' Anesthesiology Department," every patient in the world has the right to believe you are part of Cedars' team and Cedars carried an ad in The Herald. They advertise throughout South America, they said, "Come to our new modern hospital. We have all kinds of services that Cedars gives you. We have pathology for you, Cedars' pathology. We have X-rays for you, Cedars' X-rays. We have anesthesia for you, Cedars' anesthesiologists."

Dr. Cruz comes in. She makes one surgery, one operation and she goes home.

The anesthesiologist comes in the morning. They stay all day and they do procedure after procedure after procedure. They switch down there from room to room. One anesthesiologist is scheduled to do your surgery and may go next door to do somebody else and one of the other people comes in. Cedars' anesthesiologists and they give you your anesthesia. This is a very, very vital question. I urge you, as sincerely as I can, to vote that these anesthesiologists were agents, representatives, part of the Cedars' team in this case.

They gave them a free office. They gave them a secretary. They put their name on the door. They paid their phone bill, and they wanted them there on the team, in the uniform, representing and being an agent, an agent for their hospital.

This is what was going on there. The hospital provided a consent form for them. The hospital gave them their clothing, gave them an office, advertising, on and on and on.

Orlando Silva and his wife, Teresita, did not know anything about it. The Court will charge you that someone has the right to believe that they are an agent when they behave as they have here in this case.

I fear I am belaboring this, but no issue is more critical to this case than finding these anesthesiologists were agents of Cedars, and the way this case was handled and the way this business went.

Informed Consent. The doctor has a duty, under the hospital's own rules, to get an intelligent Informed Consent. That was never done in this case.

Our experts say that this is a departure form acceptable care. They violated their own rules in not getting an Informed Consent in this case.

Now, the hospital is responsible in this case. They are responsible for everything the nurses did, that they were not supposed to do, and everything those nurses should have done that they did not do.

The hospital is also responsible for Dr. Escar. The hospital is responsible for Nurse Gianniny. The hospital is responsible for Nurse Randolph and the hospital is responsible for all of their agents. All of their agents, whether it is an X-ray agent or a pathology agent or a laboratory agent or an anesthesiology agent. All of those people are on the hospital teams, seeing that those ten operating rooms go full speed every day, and I say for 5,000 operations a year.

I think Mr. Kutner and I in this case have disagreed on everything in this case except this one point, and he is in agreement with me that his people are agents of this hospital. I am sure that he will advise you of that when he gets up here to argue, that his people were agents, just like the laboratory people or the blood people or the pathology people or the X-ray people, any of those people there that were rendering these services that Cedars had advertised to the world that we give you there.

Let me leave the agency thing. I am about to get to the damage part, but I want to summarize the responsibility of Dr. Gurvich in this case, who is an agent of this hospital.

He failed to recognize and correct it. He had an esophageal intubation. He failed to recognize it and correct it. He assumed and thought that maybe he had a bronchospasm, but he did not treat that right. He put Isuprel in her stomach and that does not do anything.

Dr. Zauder, Dr. Forthman, Dr. Flor all say, "You mishandled this case. You handled it improperly and incorrectly," and he is responsible in this case and the hospital is responsible for him in this case, because he is their agent.

Let me talk about the damages, I need a drink of water bad.

What I am going to be talking about at this time is hard to talk about. You all have wondered all of the way through, I am sure, what Teresita Silva looked like. This is her wedding picture, years ago. That is Mrs. Silva. That is the lady that this lawsuit is all about. That is her husband, seated right there. Those are their four children back there (indicating).

They are citizens of this community that I represent in this awful, awful lawsuit. Here are some pictures of Dr. Silva and Mrs. Silva and some with their four children sometime back. This is the Silva family. These are in evidence and this one here is of Mrs. Silva at the beach in a bathing suit, to show you how flat her abdomen was, and when these peoples tell you that she looked like she was bout eight or nine months pregnant, that they are talking about a lady that had a flat stomach when she came into the hospital.

THE CLERK: Mr. Spence, you have used 30 minutes.

MR. SPENCE: Thank you.

The Court will give you a verdict form and His Honor will walk you through it. He will give every one of you one later on. He will explain page by page what is on this verdict form, and he will advise you that when you all go upstairs, that you are going to have an election and pick one of you to be the foreman of this case, or foreperson, decide who is going to sign it, who is going to conduct the hearing and kind of preside over your deliberations.

Then, the Judge will walk you through this and explain, question by question, what is involved, and on this verdict form, there is a place where you list the damages that are involved in this case. The damages for Dr, Silva, the damages for each of his four children, and you will remember in the voir dire a long time ago, I said, "Would you give each claim separate and individual attention? will you decide each claim that is presented here by Orlando Silva, by Landy, by Teryliz, by Carlos and by Jorge?"

Each one of these individuals has their own separate claim for their own personal loss of their mother, or in his case, his wife, and there is a verdict form here for each one of the five of them, for the past two years, what their damages have been for the past two years.

Then, there is a verdict form here for what their damages will be for the rest of their lives, and I have written in "life expectancy" here. Orlando Silva, 30 years. His son, 51 point something. Teryliz, 60. Carlos, 64. Jorge, 54, and Mrs. Silva's life expectancy is 39 years.

The Judge will tell you and ask you to take into account life expectancy, the time that is involved here and each of these children have a claim for losing their mother for the rest of their natural lives, for the rest of their lives, so you are looking at an award that takes into account, in these children's cases, 50 years, 60 years of Mother's Day rolling around, and then remembering that their mom died on Mother's Day.

These children have told you the kind of mother they had, and I will not go over it all, but that she was a wonderful woman; that she loved them all. She took good care of them. She was a pal. You could talk to her and so forth and moms, as we all know, are something special in this world. Fathers are one thing. Mothers are something quite different. They have carried that baby and brought that baby into this world, and when a child becomes a problem, nine times out of ten the child goes to the mother rather than the father and there is a very special bond and a very special relationship between a child and that child's mother.

These children got on the stand, and I cannot repeat the things that they said, that they told you about the kind of mother they had. Dr. Silva told you the kind of wife he had, and they have sustained, under the Florida law, an enormous loss. These children have lost their mother for the rest of their lives and they have been through some kind of a special torture for the last two years out there, and you may say to yourself, "Well, they should have pulled the plug," but I think the Court told you earlier on that they had a right to do what they did. They had a right to do what they did, and they have incurred a medical bill here of over $400,000 and it is in evidence. $442,537 is the hospital bill they have been sued over.

Then, there is the funeral bill here that is about $5 or $6,000, but these items are not the real damage in this case.

The Judge will explain to you that in Florida, these children and this husband are entitled to compensatory damages for the grief, the anguish, the heartbreak they have been through. The grief, the anguish, the heartbreak they have been through for the last two years.

Mrs. Silva went into that hospital the 23rd of this month. The 23rd of this month, it will be two years ago, and the big element, the big thing in this case is in assessing ample damages, enormous damages, because this is an enormous loss under the Florida law.

This is the law that the Court will give you. It is your duty to assess damages if these people were careless and the things that you have heard that they have done here; that you have an obligation to assess the damages and I am suggesting to you and recommending to you what the damages ought to be in this case.

I think each one of these claimants should receive $500,000 each for the last two years. Each one of them.

On those blanks that are there, they say "past damages" each child, and, Orlando Silva, $500,000 each for the last two years.

I recommend and urge to you that you award them compensatory damages for the future, for the rest of their lives, $2,000,000 each, for each one of the five of them. That is $10,000,000 future damages, an enormous amount of money, but this is the procedure in Florida, to award damages, compensatory damages in a wrongful death case such as this, for those elements of damage and some juror may say, "How do we figure this out, Mr. Spence?" I said, "The Judge will help you. He will give you the law on what the legal elements of damage are."

The Judge will explain to you there are five separate claims. The Judge will explain to you that there are damages awarded for the past two years, The Judge will explain to you there are damages awarded for the rest of their lives, for the rest of their lives, and it is your obligation in computing this to decide five separate claims. Give each claim separate attention, so I am going to repeat those figures.

We are asking, on behalf of these children and himself, $500,000 each for the past two years and $2,000,000 each for each one of them for the rest of their lives in the future.

Then, of course we ask that we be reimbursed for their hospital bill expense and the funeral bill.

Now, folks, I am going to sit down. I have done my best here to stay on the high road with you and talk about the key evidence in the case. Those people who were there, Dr. Escar, Mainieri, Rodriguez, Cruz, Dr, Silva. They were all there before the Code Blue was pushed. They were all there, and they told you what they saw with their own eyes and the only person that refutes that is Dr. Gurvich. He said that is not the way it was. It was some other way.

I am going to sit down. I thank you for your careful attention and when all of these lawyers have finished say what they have to say on behalf of their clients, I have a few minutes left at the tail end.

I hope you will be patient. You have been awfully patient, let me say, as I sit down.

***

THE COURT: Mr. Spence, you may proceed.

MR. SPENCE: Yes, sir.

Very briefly, folks, and I will talk quickly and we will be through and there will be no more lawyer talk, no further witnesses, no more arguments. There will be the Judge giving you the law and you all deciding in this case where the right and wrong is.

The first thing I want to draw to your attention to is this exhibit that Mr. Thompson brought over here. This is a chart that the lawyers made up. This is part of their argument. And it is a chart they made up.

And they have on here a time, 7:15, re-intubation. Now, note the time the lawyers are telling you this happened, 7:15. This exhibit is in the record and you will find it has got the torn sheet up top.

But if you will take the torn sheet and lay it right down over where it says intubation, on the sheet beneath it that is not torn, that is printed just like it. These two sheets are alike. They have all the times printed on it. And where it is torn off there, the word extubation is torn off. But read underneath it. It says intubation and it says 7:30.

Now, you have a choice. Are you going to accept Mr. Thompson's exhibit that he has made up in this trial? He asks you to believe, in all fairness he says, that the re-intubation was at 7:15. Well, they both can't be true. This is not evidence. That is evidence. And the Judge will tell you to base your decision on the evidence in the case and not what the lawyer prepared back in his office which flies in the face of what is in the record.

Now, what I am saying at this point is what we technically call rebuttal, and I only have a few minutes so I will touch on some of the things that these other lawyers have said. And I am disagreeing with them. I am rebutting them.

Number one, Mr. Sevier got a blackboard over there. And if he tells you that if you will give him these people's money, he will go out, nice guy that he is, he will go invest it in some stocks and bonds and insurance policies and he will give them the same good care with their money that the hospital gave them for his wife and their mother.

Lousy care is what he is going to give them, because his whole argument is designed to persuade you to violate your oath in this courtroom and not follow the Florida law on damages.

The Florida law on damages says these people are entitled to full, total, complete compensatory damages for their enormous loss. And if it is all the money in the world, and the loss is all the loss in the world, that is what they are entitled to. Not nickels and dimes. And not his free advice, and not his volunteering to take their money and invest it for them somewhere.

That is sheer, total nonsense. It is not the law. And Judge Testa wouldn't give you any such law as that. And we say to Mr. Sevier, "Thanks, but no thanks."

There is an issue about Dr. King in this case. And I wish it wasn't the case. But I don't know where the confusion is, but Dr. Silva and his four children say that they didn't see him there. And him saying he was there, I think that is a collateral issue and a red herring, and I would ask you to put that out of your mind. That is not what occurred in this operating room and that is not what killed Mrs. Silva; Dr. King.

And they also are on us about the court reporter. They wrote me a letter and I am supposed to take my client over there and make the corrections. And we didn't do it. And Orlando, I am sorry, that is my fault. But when they stand up here and the hospital's lawyers read out of a deposition that Dr. Silva pulled the tube out of his own wife and that was read to Dr. Silva, "Didn't you pull the tube out of your wife?" And when the hospital's lawyer reads that question, he knows that is not so. He knows that we have told them, in that second deposition, that it is full of errors and mistakes. And the hospital's lawyer knows that Dr. Gurvich pulled the tube out. And everyone in the room says that Dr, Gurvich pulled the tube out. And Dr. Gurvich, himself says he did it.

Now, would a lawyer get up here and ask him, "Didn't you say on your deposition that you pulled the tube out?" Now, is that fair? In all honesty and candor, is that fair? No, it is not.

This is a triple cheap shot. And it is designed to prejudice you against Orlando Silva and his children, just like the threats and him carrying a gun. They have told you that one time in this lawsuit that he was distressed and that he had a gun and he was going to do something. But they have told you on every opportunity, "The gun, the gun. Gun. Threat. Threat. Threat."

Why" Fairness? They want to prejudice him so bad, they want him to get short-changed in this courtroom. They want him defeated again.

They have defeated him once. They took his wife and these children's mother. And now they want to rub his nose in it and say, "Go away. You killed her. We are not responsible."

And that is just outrageous. And they are playing a little game.

Now, Mr. Thornton has stated to you that this evidence, this record is full of evidence to support a finding of agency. Mr. Kutner says that this record is full of evidence to support a finding on agency. And I feel, as I read this record, over and over and over, there is solid, firm evidence of agency.

And do you know why they are saying it? Because they don't want to pay the bill. They don't want to pay this debt. So they are saying to him, "Go away, Gurvich. You are not on our ball club. You are not on our operating room." And the truth is, Dr. Silva and his wife, neither one had anything to do with selecting the anesthesiologist. They were total strangers to them. They didn't know them.

This hospital advertised all kinds of service. Laboratory. X-ray. Drugs. Anesthesia. Surgeons or technicians. Admitting clerks. It is like going out there and getting a ticket on an airline. You get your ticket. Somebody takes your luggage, takes you to the place. Somebody gets you a drink. Somebody loads the luggage on. And they are all wearing Eastern buttons, and you don't stop them and say, "Hey, buddy, who are you? Tell me about it." It is absurd. That is all I can say.

The arrangement was such that these anesthesiologists stayed there all day. A surgeon might come in and do one surgery and leave. Ruben Gurvich stayed there all day, because that is the hospital's control over their anesthesiologists.

And I am not going to try and get into this question, but the lady comes up there, Dr. Capati, and she says, "I am Cedars' anesthesiologist. I am here to do this for you."

Any reasonable person on earth would have to say, "I take your word, Dr. Capati. You are an anesthesiologist. You are from Cedars and you are part of Cedars thing."

Just like if you come to do an X-ray of my chest or to do the blood, or you come to do anything, you are wearing a uniform. You are flying the flag and you are on the team. And you are an agent. That is the most vital issue in this case as far as this is concerned, to nail down beyond question, whether Mr. Thornton agrees to, and whether Mr. Kutner agrees to that, there is just a ton of evidence here that Ruben Gurvich was an agent. Because he was furthering the business of the hospital. And he was here in connection with the hospital's business and the hospital's interest.

And Judge Testa will read you the law on that. And he will describe it as one who holds himself out to be on the team, that the person he says that to can take their word for it. You don't have to ask him to get out a wallet and show me who you are. You are entitled to rely on the appearance and the statement, "I am part of Cedars' team. I am the anesthesiologist from Cedars' Anesthesiology Department."

And the first thing on here is if you find that Dr. Ruben Gurvich was the agent of Cedars of Lebanon, yes or no; I urge you, along with Mr. Kutner and Mr. Thornton, to vote yes on that issue. Because the evidence is overwhelming of that. No question about it. It is part of the services that were furnished. They are there all day long, had to cover those operating rooms. The whole team thing.

Now, it should be apparent to you that, because Mr. Sevier is so frightened of the agency question, that he is standing there and saying Dr. Gurvich didn't do anything wrong, because he doesn't want all of that responsibility and liability on his hospital. And Dr. Escar as well.

Now, do you find there was negligence on the part of the hospital and Dr. Escar didn't do a Code Blue and so forth, so he is in there.

Now, one other word about Dr. Gurvich's credibility. He says in his deposition, which was indeed nine hours long, that nothing on his chart, with respect to time is accurate.

"Nothing on my chart with respect to any of these times is accurate." It is all reconstruction.

But then he goes and tells his partner that he was in trouble from the beginning. In trouble from the beginning. And then he tells a different story on the chart. And then he tells a different story on the Answers to Interrogatories. And then on the deposition. So he has had about four versions for Gurvich. And which one do you want to believe?

And then there is some criticism of my hypotheticals. And I feel that this is beating a dead dog to keep talking about that.

Our hypothetical was based upon the entire deposition. If you read his deposition, Dr. Forthman, "Have you read Dr. Gurvich's deposition?" "Yes, I have read it." "What do you think about it?" "Can't be." It looks like it was cooked up, an invention. And they have just typed out a perfect alibi and put it in there.

And the torn record, they make a big deal about that. But that just shows that all of this file was in Mr. Sevier's where it went over to Mr. Kutner's. And it may be perfectly innocent. But I am saying, at one time, those two tables that are separated were one table.

And they fuss at us about sitting together. They are in bed together. The defense over here with respect to the hospital and anesthesiologists.

MR. KUTNER: I object to that statement.

THE COURT: Overruled.

MR. SPENCE: Now, Mr. Kutner doesn't like the fact that we read the deposition. He said that is a lawyer's tactic. Now, saying "tactic" makes it sound sneaky, that I did something dishonest. Well, the Judge approved of the procedure. It is a procedure under the Rules. I am entitled to do it. He, or any other lawyer, is entitled to do it. So, it is right on behalf of my client to do it in that fashion.

One other word about Mr. Kutner. Forgive me for being this blunt, but he says the damages are outrageous and insulting. Well, I find his comment about the damages outrageous and insulting. He should walk one mile with this family, one mile with this family and go see Mrs. Silva for those many months when she was in intensive care there, full of that paraphernalia in here, and those kids there everyday after school and sleeping in the hall. And he has – well, I won't say what he has, but when he says that the damages in this case are outrageous and insulting, I find that remark outrageous and insulting.

His man is going to go home and going to go back and practice anesthesiology. And his man isn't going to have any problems at all. They are without a mother. He is without his wife. And it is because it is his fault over there for a sloppy, incompetent medical care in this case.

Bronchospasm is a phony alibi. It is an invention of the flexible mind over there. There was no bronchospasm in this case. Zauder says there wasn't. Wright says there wasn't. And all of these other people tell you there is no such animal as a bronchospasm that doesn't respond to drugs and only ends after·the patient dies. It is fantastic to suggest that alibi and defense to you.

One last thing. He keeps saying that Dr. Silva interfered, that he came in there, kicked his shoes off and interfered and killed his wife. Arostegui says that he took the stethoscope, jerked it away from Dr. Gurvich and listened to his wife's chest for two minutes. Mr. Grossman had us time the two minutes, and it seemed like forever. This doctor takes his wife's breath sounds with a stethoscope in two or three seconds. He doesn't need any two minutes. So when Arostegui walks in here, part of the hospital's team, and says that, it is with design. It is with plan. And it is for a purpose. It is for the purpose of besmirching Dr. Silva. All of those things thrown in there; killing his wife, interfering with her, wouldn't give her Aminophylline. But that is a useless drug in cardiac arrest.

So, we have just had to live with the phantoms here. Just, you know, squirt one up in the air here and there. And you have to keep knocking them down to try and get the truth on top of the table.

I am down to the end. I want to talk about the damages one minute and sit down. Dr. Orlando Silva, Landy, Teryliz, Carlos and Jorge, will be sitting right here at this table, waiting for your verdict in this case, and your verdict in this case will, in truth, be based on the law and the evidence. And they will be waiting for a verdict that says to them, "You lost your mother, you lost your wife, because of carelessness and we are going to hold these Defendants responsible for your loss. And because your loss is enormous and great, the damages have to be enormous and great."

My final sentence: Mother. I do believe that most people would say that a mother's love is the greatest love on earth. I mean, fellows fall in love with girls. People get married. And people love each other for lots of reasons, but I dare say that the greatest philosophers of all times, the Bible and on and on, will tell you that there is nothing quite so precious and real forever in one's life and in these children's lives as their mother's love. And not having that love, and not having her here is what this case is about.

Go do your job, please. Okay?

Verdict: $4.1 million

ISBN 1-41205257-2

227914

Made in the USA